THE GENIE IN THE BOTTLE

Unraveling the Myths About Wine

Roger Morris

A&W Publishers, Inc.
New York

Published by
A & W Publishers, Inc.
95 Madison Avenue
New York, New York 10016

Designed by *Paul Chevannes*

Library of Congress Number: 80-70367
ISBN: 0-89104-198-2

Printed in the United States of America

Acknowledgements

I thank my wife, Ella, who gives me good counsel and helps me keep my writing in perspective; my brother, Ed, who led me into a career of writing; and Jan Penix Mayhew, teacher and friend, who listened and taught me the snowball theory.

Professionally, fond thanks to Abby Chapple, an excellent editor who gave me my first breaks as a freelancer and as a wine writer; two current editors, John Montorio and Bill Tudor, who believe the best writer-editor relationship is for the former to meet deadlines and the latter to get checks out promptly; and to my agent, Phil Spitzer, and my book editor, Ruth Pollack, who makes publishing seem easy.

Finally, there are some winemakers whose give-and-take during interviews convinced me that I was in the right business—notably, Bob Mondavi, Ham Mowbray, Paul Draper, and Warren Winiarski. They must be held partially accountable.

Contents

CONTENTS

Introduction

A year or so ago, I was at a tasting at the Sheraton Carlton Wine Bar in Washington, D.C., scribbling some notes about an Inglenook Charbono when this interesting woman approached me in the corner and asked if I were with the trade.

"No," I replied, "I write about wine."

"Oh really," she said, "for whom?"

When I explained that I had been the wine columnist for *The Washington Star* for three years, she exclaimed, "Oh, you're Roger Morris! We've always wondered who you were because no one had ever met you. We figured you were some conservative gentleman living on his estate out in the Virginia countryside."

None of the suspicions were even remotely true.

Some time and a few glasses of wine later I was to tell the woman, Jo Hawkins, herself an excellent wine writer, the truth. I am a born-again wine drinker, business executive, and freelance writer. Since I had never specialized before, and since I had only been a serious wine drinker for a few years, I was frankly afraid that my ignorance would be found out in the presence of other wine professionals.

Not that I didn't trust my writing. With my freelance experience, a modicum of research that any writer does, plus what I always thought was a good palate, I had little doubt that my columns would stand on their own.

I was not so sure that I could do as well.

But the primary reason I cowered in the closet was that I really didn't want to be influenced by other writers. Most wine books I had read were written either by Europeans or Californians, neither covering the others' territory very well. Additionally, even in my formative bottles, I had a feeling that what I was reading in the books had limited applicability to what I was buying in the stores and tasting at home.

It was not that all the books were the same. But it did seem as though every writer started out with a set of *a priori* approaches. The geography of wine, the material that had to be obligatorily included in a wine book, the etiquette of wines, the tasting of wines—all seem to be agreed upon. What each writer would do was to cover this material and then focus on one aspect of this spectrum.

I am sometimes a brash person . . . but I am a *conservative* brash person. So let me say that probably eighty to ninety percent of what has been written is sound, and I have no desire to question it. I will not try to pull any rabbits out of the bottle.

However, I do believe that while I was in the closet (much less dramatic than Moses' mountain), I developed in my columns, and hence in this book, three perspectives that I think are important and which might in some instances be different from those of my colleagues.

• One is that the wine world is changing much more rapidly than most of us imagine, and we writers have to recognize this by gambling in print with our opinions.

• Two is that there are some traditional wisdoms that

have to be challenged, again at some risk to the writer, no matter who believes them and how many hundreds of years old they are.

• Third is that readers need to be more involved in what we're writing. Jim Lucas of Fromm & Sichel calls it "accessibility," and he is probably right. I think wine can be demystified without shaking its foundations. Things can be made *simpler*, if not *simple*, for the drinker. Additionally, some fun and puns can fly about while the demystification is taking hold.

So when I defined fairly early in my wine writing days what I wanted to do in my columns, I put them in this order—1) Involve, 2) Entertain, 3) Educate, 4) Recommend, 5) Sit in judgment.

I expected to get positive reactions from what I saw as the primary audience—people who drink a lot of wine and know something about varietals but have not had the time or interest to become experts. Personally, I love reading what experts say about technical topics, but I'm not sure that most wine readers do unless it is directly applicable to their drinking.

Anyway, I had little hope that wine professionals—the winemakers on one side and the drinkers with the 5,000-bottle cellars on the other—would care much for my approach. After all, I have theories about baseball, too, such as that hitters' averages and productivity would rise if they hit away and did not take the first pitch religiously, if they did not play hit-and-run, or tried to pull the ball. Since most Little Leaguers are taught all these things, it is doubtful that many baseball men, in their maturity, would even consider such simplistic notions.

Nor did I think that winemakers who had gone to the University of California at Davis and elsewhere would challenge such truisms as you can still get the full impact of the wine (except the inebriation) if you spit it out.

I have been pleasantly surprised. No one seems all that

distraught that I challenge some theories or that I write in a very casual (if sometimes impassioned) manner about their livelihood or, in the case of the wine buff, fantasies. A true rabble rouser would be crushed. I am delighted. Perhaps I had some judgmental capabilities in addition to a writing style and a palate.

So, whether you're new to wine or have enjoyed it for many more years than I have, here is what I hope to provide in this book:

First, I think that geography, labels, and appellation laws take up far too much space in most wine books. I will pass over them briefly and get to the matter at hand—tasting wine, enjoying what is tasted, and understanding that taste. If this moves you to think about something you have not thought about before, or to try something that you have ignored, then my primary purpose will have been served.

Part of that thinking also involves my second purpose. I hope that those of you who are experienced will consider some of the arguments made against traditional wisdoms. This is minor to the book in terms of pages, but major in concept in places. (In other places, incidentally, you will find me terribly orthodox.)

Finally, I hope you enjoy the stylistic approach. Few of us sit in a wing chair before a butler-stoked fire in our silken robe, drinking a glass of fine vintage Port—yet most books seem to be written with that in mind.

Another story: A young man who took one of my wine classes approached me following the first lecture, saying that the class wasn't what he and his wife expected. As the class was for beginners, but nevertheless had some wine-merchant types in it, I asked:

"Why, isn't it sophisticated enough or technical enough?"

"Oh no," he exclaimed, "but we read your columns, and, well, we sort of expected that you would be doing everything except leaping into walls "

Wait 'til next time around.

PART ONE
The Three Steps

Chapter One

Tasting the good taste

WHEN I was a kid growing up in the hollows of West Virginia, I hated practically every type of food that wasn't meat and potatoes. Once, according to mom, an aunt who was babysitting allowed me to gorge myself at a tender age on fried hog liver. It made me so ill that I never wanted to eat any kind of liver again.

I also went through my teen years not liking green salads, lamb, fish (saltfish and sardines had been my only exposure), and any number of perfectly normal foods. My gastronomic Index was as formidable as the literary one the Vatican still kept in those days.

The situation was not hopeless. My wife, attempting a cultural turnaround not unlike the engineer's feat in *Trail of the Lonesome Pine*, gradually enticed, cajoled, and threatened me into eating salads. Gradually, all the other taboos fell away. *Foie gras* is now music to my mouth. In fact, paralleling the book, my wife is now the conservative partner: escargots, sushi, and steak tartare remain ordeals for her.

But we are now four paragraphs into a wine book and still talking about food. Recently I was at a captains-of-industry dinner in New York, and one acquaintance was fretting over whether he should have a white wine served at the head table so that his boss, who detested red wine, would have something to wash down the bits of beef filet.

Another friend, a gourmet cook, practically goes into convulsions that seem to be stolen from *The Exorcist* whenever a dessert wine is hinted.

And a third friend whom I had plied with Champagne from time to time confessed that she really didn't care for it—would I try a white Burgundy instead?

People who would never turn their noses up at exotic cooking think nothing of rejecting whole glasses of wine out of hand (or mouth as the case is). Most likely, their reasoning is no more sound than mine was with liver—they had a bad experience—or, worse, they have a fear of trying. To really enjoy wines, you first have to have the right attitude, which is simply, "I'll give it a try." And it should be an objective try.

After attitude comes knowing what to look for—and we'll get to that in a few pages. These two things, an adventurous spirit and a knowing what to look for, are more important than memorizing regions, learning to tell your Brix from your Oechsle, or mastering the languages of the label. After all, there are a lot of sexually fulfilled people out there who have never mastered Johnson, peeked at *Penthouse*, or sought comfort with Alex.

You don't even need to know how wine is made, but a few words here might give some meaning to your drinking. Ripe grapes have various flavors, acids, and sugars, and, once crushed, their juice is fermented by aid of yeast, either without the skins (generally the case with white wines) or with the skins (generally the case for reds). The red coloring, incidentally, comes from the skins and not the juice, with only minor exceptions.

4

During fermentation, sugar turns to alcohol, so that the finished wine will have flavors, alcohol, acid, and various degrees of sweetness.

The wines that are dryer, that is, less sweet, are generally table wines or wines we drink with foods. Those that have a good deal of sweetness are generally dessert or after-dinner wines. Fortified wines are wines that have alcohol—often brandy—added, and, depending on sweetness, can be enjoyed before or after dinner. Finally, we have sparkling wines, that is, ones with all those bubbles caused by having the wine continue to ferment after it is bottled. Sparkling wines can be drunk any time, fairly much a matter of personal preference.

(Those of you who know something about wine are probably saying, "Jesus, I've had about enough of this simple rhetoric." Patience. It takes four years for a Cabernet Sauvignon vine to produce usable grapes.)

Now that you know in the simplest forms the types of wine you will be tasting, how do you approach tasting? Surprisingly, many wine people have horrible palates and have difficulty in telling their acid from sugar. Others in the trade know a hell of a lot about wine, but don't really know how to get the most out of it.

There is no *one* way to taste, but let me suggest *a* way to taste, some of which may be heresy to the orthodoxy. First of all, forget color. Color can give you keys to wine, but nothing that you can't find out better in the taste, which itself is a combination of nose and mouth. Color does add to the enjoyment, but so does the label and the companion and the food—but you don't judge a wine's *taste* on the basis of those extraneous items, either.

So taste a wine thusly: Fill less than a quarter of a stemmed glass and swirl it around gently. This does two things: it will liberate mustiness from a wine that has not been properly aired, and it will release the fragrances of the wine. You smell, looking for fruit, floweriness, and complexity.

Next take a sip. Swish it around your mouth, up over the roof, and down under the tongue. Forget about those drawings of the mouth with arrows pointing to "sweet," "bitter," "salt," and so on—I hope that no one has put salt in your wine. The primary thing here is to notice the flavors and complexity of the wine, which we will discuss in a moment. Swallow, and note the taste on swallowing. Now, take another sip and form a trough of your tongue, allowing the wine to languish, trembling in the middle, as you gently breathe air in over it, inhaling the rich mixture into your lungs. As a warning, you should try the exercise with water first, or else you'll choke and look like a sperm whale spewing Pouilly-Fuissé across the living room. This process is called "whistling in" a wine, and the purpose is to bring wine gases into the lungs and out again to be evaluated along with the tastes you get in swallowing the wine.

It works partially. Many, if not most, top wine people will not swallow the wine, but will whistle it in and then spit out the wine. It keeps them clear of head and prevents them from swallowing a lot of raw or young wine that is being evaluated. It also makes them miss part of the taste of wine—the aftertaste, which you can get only from swallowing a wine and then exhaling.

Anyway, I cast my vote with owner Joseph Phelps who once commented to me as Walter Schug, the talented winemaker at Joseph Phelps, was spitting out some wine: "That's one thing I've never learned how to do."

But all of this swallowing, sniffing, whistling, and spitting does you no good if you don't know what to look for. Let me suggest nine items to evaluate, which for the amateur may seem like an excessive number and for the connoisseur a too meager number.

1. *Flavors.* We can talk about esters and such, but essentially what we are seeking is to know what the wine tastes *like.* And the word "like" generally means comparison—*like*

berries, peaches, violets, road tar, geraniums, whatever. At this point, we are not interested in the origin of the flavors.

2. *Tannin*. Tannin is that bitterness around your tongue and even coating your front teeth which tastes like the hulls of shelled pecans. Sometimes it is dusty, and sometimes it is fairly sharp. Tannin comes primarily from grape skins and seeds—pips—and helps preserve a wine and make it complex, which is one reason we note it in our tasting. Since only red wines have prolonged skin contact, we note little or no tannin in white wines.

3. *Sweetness*. Or dryness. This does not necessarily mean an exact registering of how much sugar is in a wine, but how sweet it tastes. Confused? Go to Number 4.

4. *Acid*. The sharpness or "clearing" that you get shortly after you register sweetness is acid. Ideally, a wine with a lot of sugar will have a lot of acid for balance. That way, you can taste a sweet German Riesling wine and not tire of it because, after the rich nectar flavors and the full sweetness, the acid present will balance this sweetness and thus "clear" the palate as you swallow.

5. *Fullness and feel*. The tactile value of a wine must be measured, and it is often the result of sugar, alcohol, and glycerine. All three will make a wine seem more substantial, chewy, and pliable. This may or may not be desired, depending on the type of wine. A Muscadet is not expected to be full, while a white Burgundy should be almost luscious.

6. *Balance*. A good wine is balanced in two ways: the sugar and acid are harmony, as are the flavors (or fruit) and tannin in red wines. The better the balance, the better the wine.

7. *Complexity*. A wine may have one great flavor and still not be a great wine. As with a woman (or man, depending on your preference), a great wine is complex and shows you several different levels of attraction. The test is easy: as you smell, then taste, a wine, ask if the aromas and flavors change as the wine progresses through your mouth (liquid)

and nose (gases)? If so, it has different levels and is thus complex.

8. *Maturity*. Some examples: a young wine may have potential, yet it might taste bitter, with little evidence of fruit; a mature Burgundy may be mellow and velvety, in perfect harmony; an old Bordeaux may taste slightly "brown" or meaty, still good, but over the hill. Part of tasting any wine is determining whether it is before, at, or past its prime.

9. *Apparent flaws*. So far, we have been speaking positively, but some wines have flaws that are noticeable to most anyone. One flaw is that the wine may be vinegary or have too much acid. There may be aromas of sulfur. It may lack acid and disappear immediately from the palate. Whatever the fault or the cause, it should be noted by the taster.

Not all of these nine points of tasting can be developed overnight. You have to practice, practice, practice. As you practice, you learn more by reading and studying.

But the best study of all is critically drinking what's in the bottle.

Chapter Two

The major varietals

RECENTLY some friends in the wine trade were finishing off a long summer's afternoon of informal sampling by trying out the new Taylor California Cellars line of varietal wines.

"The Chardonnay doesn't taste like Chardonnay," one of them muttered. "It has none of the traits. In fact, it tastes like a Chenin Blanc." Another enjoyed the taste of the Zinfandel; however, it came across more like a "gutsy Beaujolais."

Nor is the question of varietal integrity limited to the lower end of the price line. For example, I fancy the Paul Draper Selections for Havelock Gordon, but I found the Chardonnay and Zinfandel unconventional in style.

Varietal traits—what a wine from a particular grape variety should taste like—is often confusing not only for the beginning drinker but also to many people skiing along on the intermediate slurps as well.

Most prominent grape varieties produce wines that have certain classical characteristics or traits which are generally

9

common to all those wines. When we see the word *Gewürz-traminer*, for example, we may not know how good or how bad that wine will taste, nor do we know *exactly* how it will taste. But we should have an idea. Having said that, there are any number of reasons why what we expect may not be what we get.

Things that may influence or change varietal characteristics include blending, degree of ripeness of grapes, age of the wine, soil and climate, fermentation techniques, aging with or without wood, age of the wine when consumed, and clones. A Pinot Noir may be a Pinot Noir may be a Pinot Noir, but not all clones are created (or taste) equal.

Demurs aside, we can cite certain varietal traits wine drinkers may want to memorize (both in word and taste) as an aid to understanding what they drink.

Beginning with whites, probably the most distinctive taste belongs to the Riesling, also known in California as the White or Johannisberg (never Grey) Riesling. Although the wine can be fermented very dry (particularly in Alsace) or very sweet (in California and Germany), most Rieslings give off an aroma and taste that is fruity and flowery, or, in a word, nectary. Sweeter Rieslings also have at times a distinctive oily or petroleum smell, which, when in proper balance, is a good indication of richness.

Almost as distinctive is the Gewürztraminer of Alsace and California, which, sweet or dry, is definitely spicy. No other word for it. If you had to reach for a particular spice, I suppose cloves would be as close as any.

Perhaps the greatest, and certainly most versatile, white is the Chardonnay of California, Chablis, Champagne, and white Burgundy, including Côte d'Or (Montrachet) and Mâcon (Pouilly-Fuissé). A Chardonnay has a certain broad vegetable smell and taste (such as a corn leaf), a rounded, fruitiness (as one might get from green apples or the aroma of an eau-de-vie), and a definite richness and fullness, particularly in Burgundy. It often has tastes of lemon and vanilla, partially from oak aging, and a butteriness (not quite like caramel), particularly in Burgundy. It can even have a definite earthiness. A Chardonnay should never be flowery or nectary.

Another herbal or herbaceous grape is the Sauvignon Blanc of the Upper Loire (Pouilly Fumé, Sancerre), Bordeaux (at its heights in Graves), and California (where it is also known as Fumé Blanc). If a distinction is to be made between the vegetable tastes of Chardonnay and of Sauvignon Blanc, the latter would be tarter (grassy, even sour grass). Sometimes there can be a smokiness to Fumé wines, and often a thin one can have an unpleasant nail polish or aldehyde aroma.

Getting back to fruit, there is the Chenin Blanc, which can be made sweet or dry. Okay, so a Riesling is fruity, too. The difference? A Riesling can approach the richness of a peach or fragrant apples. Without being overly grapy, the Chenin Blanc is closer to the fruitiness of a light, white table grape. It is definitely less nectary.

With the greatest red, Cabernet Sauvignon, the words that leap to mind are green olives or vegetal (like chewing on a green fruit stem), blackcurrants, and bitter (as in tannin). These are the wines of Napa and Bordeaux and practically every place else in the grape-growing world. Cabernet may also have a minty or eucalyptus taste (California), an almost-sweet taste (young Margaux), and a "bricky" or "stony" undertaste (Graves).

A Pinot Noir, on the other hand, is more voluptuous and earthy. In fact, it can even taste earthy. It may have a pungent or gamy taste and aroma which can produce a marvelous aftertaste. Pinot Noirs generally have less acid and less tannin than Cabernet, hence a certain fatness. An old Burgundy, such as a Corton, has a full, woodsy, organic richness that a Cabernet cannot approach.

From the Rhône comes Syrah. Also earthy, but often with a blackberry nose when young and a smell of road tar when old. And if you swallow that last sip, then swallow again, you can get the taste of a dark cherry as you roll the pit around in your mouth.

Gamay, the grape of Beaujolais, is fruity in the grapy sense. It can be almost soda-pop-like in its aroma, and its freshness is to be valued.

Finally, the Zinfandel of California. Although there are many roads to Zin, I look for an assertive berry smell and flavor, a Port-like mahogany taste, and, sometimes, a corn-oil richness.

If you'd like to do your own cross-varietal tasting, one way would be to line up, in the order presented above, a Bernkasteler Kabinett, Alsatian Gewürztraminer, Robert Mondavi Chardonnay, white Graves, Vouvray, Jordan Cabernet, Davis Bynum Pinot, Crozes-Hermitage, Beaujolais-Villages, and a Ridge Zinfandel. I may get some arguments on choice, but at least they won't bankrupt you.

When you've got the varietal tastes memorized, don't get hung up on varietal purity. You shouldn't kick a spunky alley cat because he doesn't look Persian.

Chapter Three

The geography of wine

LIKE generals of great armies, whose maps could not chart climates or the vagaries of terrain, many wine drinkers launch into reading about wines of a particular country only to become mired in history, obscure appelations, and fermentation techniques.

They retreat in panic, sometimes falling back as far as the Almadén Bottleneck.

A disclaimer: I love digging into the lore of a particular wine, generally after I've just purchased a bottle. At the same time, I feel a quick overview is the best approach at this juncture as we march to unravel the mysteries of wine. Once we have the big picture, other books can provide all the intimate snapshots.

So let's begin with one fact. The three countries that provide the widest variety of superior table wines are France, the United States, and Italy, probably in that order. The United States is more like France, while Italy is like neither and is still waiting to produce really great white wines.

13

What about Germany? It produces great Rieslings, and we thank the Lord for that, but it produces little else.

Spain has some excellent table and fortified wines, as does Portugal. Australia and South Africa have their moments. Eastern Europe and South America will never run dry.

Yet, France, the United States, and Italy stand above all. We will begin with France.

• *France.* There are eight primary regions: Bordeaux, Burgundy (including the Mâconnais and the Côte Chalonnaise), Chablis (sometimes considered a part of Burgundy), Champagne (sparkling only), the Loire Valley, the Rhône Valley, Beaujolais (also considered a part of Burgundy), and Alsace.

Bordeaux produces great red wines made primarily from Cabernet Sauvignon (Médoc, Graves areas) and Merlot (Pomerol, St.-Emilion), great white wines made of Sauvignon Blanc and Semillon (Graves), and great dessert wines, also made from Sauvignon Blanc and Semillon (Sauternes and Barsac). Sometimes the wines are known by their communes—for example, Margaux, St.-Estèphe, and Paulliac are all communes of the Médoc, or, more specifically, the Haut-Médoc.

More than 100 years ago, the wines of the Médoc—the great Clarets as the English dubbed them—were classified according to the price they fetched (which was assumed to be an indication of quality) with the *premier crus*, or "great growths" being awarded to four *châteaux*—Ch. Lafite-Rothschild, Ch. Margaux, Ch. Haut-Brion (actually in Graves), and Ch. Latour.

A few years ago Ch. Mouton-Rothschild politicked itself onto the list. There are dozens of lesser growths of varying quality, and there are lists of them in standard wine books should you have a fetish for memorization. However, it is better to taste and note or to take recommendations of wine merchants and experts, as the lists are a bit archaic.

Mis en bouteilles au château means the wine is estate-bottled, that is, it was bottled where the grapes were grown. This is not *necessarily* a sign of quality although it tends to be. The alternative is a shipper's wine, wherein a company such as B&G or Calvet have purchased young wines from a number of *châteaux* and then blended and aged under their own labels. Many of these are very good buys.

Burgundy prime is divided into three: the Côte d'Or to the north, the Mâconnais in the south, and the Côte Chalonnaise in the middle. The Côte d'Or is where the great wines are produced from minuscule vineyards: the great reds come from the northern half (Côte de Nuits) of the "golden slope" and the great whites from the southern half (Côte de Beaune).

The grape of the great reds is Pinot Noir—one French achievement California is having problems duplicating—and the grape of the great whites is Chardonnay. Burgundy also has the *cru* system, although estate bottling on these garden-sized plots is more imagination than reality. What *is* reality is that Burgundy whites and reds can be stupendous. Unfortunately, the quality has fallen overall in recent years, and many wines produced during the "great" year of 1976 should have their pedigrees lifted.

The stepchildren of Burgundy are the red wines of the Mâconnais, often named after a town (Mercurey, Givry) and the whites of the Côte Chalonnaise, also often named after a town, including that Cinderella wine that should have its glass slipper downsized, Pouilly-Fuissé.

Chablis, some distance from Burgundy proper, should be considered a separate area, although it does derive its reputation from the great Burgundian white grape, the Chardonnay. The similarity ends there, as Chablis can be crisp and flinty, while the great Meursaults and Montrachets of the Côte d'Or are rich and luscious. The *cru* system exists here also.

Champagne? The original sparkler which has a lot of crummy imitations bearing its name. Champagne is made of Pinot Noir and Chardonnay grapes, generally blended and produced by great Champagne houses (Moët et Chandon, Bollinger). The manner of production is described in the chapter on sparkling wines.

The Loire Valley is noted for three areas and three grapes. At the head of the valley, Sauvignon Blanc reigns with the tart, vegetal wines of Sancerre and Pouilly Fumé. Downstream is Vouvray with its slightly blowsy, semi-sweet wines made from Chenin Blanc. At the mouth of the Loire is Muscadet, whose primary grape, the Melon, produces a crisp wine that is neither very vegetal nor fruity, but which has a nice, crisp body that could be called a poor man's Chablis.

The Rhône Valley consists primarily of great reds and adequate whites. The greatest reds are in the northern half and are made of the Syrah grape, whose wines can taste of road tar and blackberries. Hermitage, Côte Rôtie, Cornas, and St.-Joseph are made primarily from the Syrah.

The other famous Rhône wine is a true Mediterranean wine made from an assortment of grapes. I give you the moderate-bodied and now moderate-quality Châteauneuf-du-Pape. Also look in the Rhône for the rosés of Tavel and the light reds called simply Côtes du Rhône made from Grenache, Cinsault, and other workhorse grapes that impart a fresh, peppery taste.

Beaujolais, whose fruity, fresh reds once owned our hearts, is made from the Gamay grape. Chill it slightly and drink it young. There are some longer-lasting wines from a dozen plus villages which can use their own names: Morgon, Saint-Amour, Brouilly, and so on.

Finally Alsace, the only region in France where the grape variety-as-wine-name prevails. The grapes—Gewürztraminer, Riesling, Sylvaner—are made into crisp wines.

• *United States.* Practically all premium wines are known by the variety of grape, which makes things easy. What makes it hard is that a single winery may produce a dozen different varieties.

Napa and Sonoma are the established, quality regions that

can successfully grow practically every grape made famous by France and Germany, and even some by Italy. Many new regions—or newly rediscovered regions—such as Monterey, Amador, and Santa Clara are establishing themselves as premium territories.

Other prime regions of the United States are New York (still keeping company with the common tramp—the grapy American varietals), the Middle Atlantic states (particularly Maryland), and the Northwest (Washington, Oregon).

So, from a geographical and labeling standpoint, the new kid at the cuvée, the United States, is fairly easy to understand in its simplicity—but difficult to keep up with in its diversity.

• *Italy.* Italy is the sleeping beauty of the wine world. It is the ancient of ancients when it comes to wine production, but it is just now becoming seriously known for the complexity and diversity of its wines.

As one would expect with such a venerable producer of wines and one not historically worried about the strictures of labeling as have been the French and Germans, its system is one of chaos. Some wines are known by the grape variety, some by the town or region, and some by a descriptive or historic name. For example, we have Nebbiolo (a variety), Chianti (a region), and Lacrima Christi (a description—the tears of Christ).

The primary growing areas of Italy lie in the northern and central sections of the country. The reds here are known for their intensity, longevity, and, sometimes, fairly high acidity, while the whites are known for their earthy generosity. The best grapes of Italy are the Nebbiolo or Spanna, which is responsible for the great red wines of the Piedmont, and the Sangiovese, a primary grape of the great Chiantis of Tuscany. Other major areas are Verona and the Alto Adige.

• *Germany.* Along the Rhine and Moselle (or Mosel) grow some of the world's greatest grapes under some of the most trying conditions—a cold climate and steep hillside. From these grapes come the great white dessert wines of Germany. The truly dry or table wines account for only about 15 percent of Germany's white wine production, and its red wine is negligible in quality and quantity, due to the northern climate.

With so little (and yet so much) to work with, the Germans have come up with a very complicated system. Let's take it step by step. The five great growing regions are Mosel-Saar-Ruwer, the Rheingau, the Rheinpfalz (or Palatinate), the Rheinhessen, and the Nahe.

The principal grape is Riesling, and the label will generally carry the grape variety whether it's Riesling or not. In fact, the label tells you everything. As to where the wine comes from within the individual region—well, you'll just have to sit down with your atlas and memorize which is which. There are large districts, towns, individual vineyards, and collections of vineyards, but it is difficult to tell by the label which is which and which is prized. Sorry, but that's the way it is. You have to look it up.

One thing that you used to be sure of was how sweet the wine would be. The minimum designation of quality is *QmP* or *Qualitätswein mit Prädikat*. The basic grade within QmP is *Kabinett*, and—going up the scale of sweetness—*Spätlese, Auslese, Beerenauslese*, and *Trockenbeerenauslese*. Essentially, each step up in grade means more sugar and hence more sweetness.

The problem today, however, is how much of that sugar has been converted into alcohol (traditionally eight to ten percent) and how much is left for sweet, nectary goodness. Since most of the world drinks table and not dessert wines, German wineries are increasingly trying to shift a major portion of their production into the drier area. This causes a problem for label readers, as the spätlesen (the plurals take an "n") and other designations have to do with "must weight," that is, roughly, the amount of sugar *before* fermentation and not sugar in the bottle.

Hence, today it is possible to have an Auslese trocken—a

dry wine of fairly high alcohol because the bulk of the sugar has been converted to alcohol and not left as residual sugar.

The key? Look at three things—the QmP category, which will indicate the original amount of sugar in the grapes; the percentage of alcohol (the higher, the less sugar left over); and the designation "trocken" or "dry" on the label.

• *Other Countries.* It is a shame to kiss off in a few words the great wines and regions of other countries, but it will be a loving kiss. Spain is known primarily for its excellent reds and so-so whites from the Rioja region and its magnificent fortified Sherries of Jerez. Portugal is also famous for its fortified wines—Port from the Douro and Madeira from the island of the same name. Additionally, there are the "green" wines, both white and red, or *vinho verdes*, and the fairly good reds of Dão.

In Eastern Europe, look to the wines of Hungary, Austria, and Romania. In middle Europe the lovely whites of Switzerland. In Africa, the prime production is at the southern tip of the continent—the wines of South Africa. Australia has a fine wine industry. In South America, Chile and Argentina produce some excellent wines and excellent values.

How do you ever learn all of these places, labels, grapes, and designations? You won't. No one will entirely. My recommendations are these. First, get comfortable with tasting and the basics of wine. Then read about the regions of the United States, France, Italy, and Germany while you explore their readily available wines. Finally, branch out by buying wines from other countries and then looking up the individual wines. To me, this makes more sense than reading about the wines of the Paarl or Hunter Valley—and then not being able to find them on the shelf. You thus have no taste to match with your knowledge, and you soon forget what you've read.

In sum, buy first, and then read *as* you drink. Who cares if you get a few wine spots on the map of Corsica?

PART TWO
Developing a Wine Sense

Chapter Four

Experiments with a bottle

ANYONE interested in learning more about wine understandably searches out wine books, goes to tastings, and perhaps even takes a class in some aspect of oenology. That is all to the good, but there are some fundamental lessons for beginners that can be learned privately over a few weekends with the help of a few inexpensive bottles of wine.

First is the lesson of blending. One evening for example, we were having a London broil for dinner, so I chose a bottle of Bordeaux of the 1974 vintage which was just coming onto the market—a Château de Pez—reputable enough in most cases. I was not in the Médoc during the harvest of '74, but, after a taste of the wine, I would bet that de Pez picked early in fear of rain. There was a definite taste of unripe grapes, astringent and bitter.

Setting the bottle aside, I opened a 1973 Beaulieu Burgundy, which proved acceptable though bland. The remainder of that bottle was recorked and also set aside. Two days later, I mixed the two in a glass, a practice that is often shunned because the drinker is getting away from the true nature of the wine as the vintner intended it.

In this case, the sum of the de Pez and the Beaulieu was considerably better than the individual parts. The blandness of the latter was overcome, while the bitterness of the former became a pleasant tannic tug of aftertaste. In this manner, I gradually finished off both bottles.

Thus, by first tasting two individual wines and then blending them, one can better understand the counterbalancing forces of wine: acid versus sugar, tannin versus fruit. We can also better appreciate the art of the *négociant-éleveur* who buys casks of raw wine from lesser holdings in the Bordeaux and elsewhere and by blending and tasting, blending and testing, comes up with very good, if never great, wines. In fact, while a classified vineyard might suffer during a particular year, a blended or "shipper's" wine can often overcome the ill effects of a poor vintage.

A second lesson from the bottle is that of oxidation and aging. A handsome lad of twenty may look worn and dissipated at fifty—age has been cruel. A gawky gal of twenty may turn into a charming and sophisticated woman of fifty—age has been kind. So it is with wine.

Begin your lesson by leaving some wine in a bottle after the first go around. Recork it, of course, and keep it at room temperature, if red, and in the most temperate part of the refrigerator, if white. The white may prove to age poorly as oxygen takes hold, becoming cantankerous and acidy. The red may improve for several days as the tanning mellows and the fruit blossoms.

By such testing, a taster can learn by seeing what time and oxygen do to individual elements of a wine. Within limits, one can also learn to tell how a particular wine will age and for approximately how long it will keep or improve.

Third is the lesson that temperature plays. We know the rules of thumb which have us serve most reds at room temperature and most whites chilled. We also know that a few reds, such as Beaujolais, are generally lightly chilled. There are a number of reasons why this is so, but have you ever tried to find out why? A friend of mine who is fond of a particular brand of inexpensive Côtes-du-Rhône prefers it refrigerated because the coolness hides some minor flaws. Conversely, I often prefer some Beaujolais, such as a Morgon, at room temperature, so that its Burgundy-like assertiveness is not dulled.

There are more complicated reasons of acids and fruitiness, and there are limits to applications (I have yet to meet anyone who enjoys a warm Moselle), but temperature testing is another fertile area of learning and experimentation.

The pairing of wine to food is a fourth lesson. Mutton goes with Bordeaux, game with Burgundy, we read. And memorize. But do we understand why?

Try this. Open a bottle of chilled Moselle Kabinett and a chilled bottle of Chablis some evening when you have a refrigerator full of leftovers. Work your way through testing each wine against each food. Cheese. Tuna fish. Cold chicken. A pork chop. Vanilla cookie. Which wine goes best, and are there instances where neither fits? Do the same with other wines. Gradually, you learn why a certain wine works because it balances an element of food—such as fat— or complements something—such as spiciness.

Finally, there is the lesson of memory. Open a Zinfandel from California, a Bardolino from Italy, a Côtes-de-Nuits from Burgundy. Taste each, concentrating, but taking no notes. Recork. Try again an hour later, striving to recall the bouquet, taste, and aftertaste before you sip each. Have a bottle of Fumé Blanc for dinner one night and another bottle of the same the next night. Again, try to remember before tasting. Gradually, you train yourself to have a wine memory, just as you have one with food. Notes are necessary, but sometimes we depend too greatly on them.

The rewards of taking the time to experiment with wine are that you don't have to depend on books to remember which wine goes with a new dish or how long a tannic bottle of Bordeaux should age in the cellar. Your senses will guide you to what works and what fails.

Chapter Five

Comparing two bottles

NOT long ago, Sterling Vineyards caused a bit of commotion when it pitted its 1974 Merlot against a 1974 Chateau Petrus, a great vineyard from Pomerol, a region of Bordeaux wherein the Merlot grape is predominant. A panel of tasters preferred the Sterling, of course, else we might never have heard about the contest through huge newspaper ads. The Sterling wine *is* delicious and less expensive although 1974 was hardly a good year to show the best that Petrus has.

Head-to-head competition is an everyday pastime for us aggressive Americans, whether it is Alabama against Penn State, Billy Jean King against Bobby Riggs, or Perrier against Evian. But we lose some of the lesson of competition if we only concentrate on which of the two is better. Instead, we should occasionally look at the match for what it tells us about the competitors, as John McPhee did in comparing tennis players Ashe and Graebner in his excellent book, *Levels of the Game.*

So it is with wine. Looking into the soul of one bottle is a profitable undertaking. So is comparing six or eight bottles during a tasting. But perhaps the most instructive activity is comparing two bottles, whether you are trying to learn tasting characteristics, regional differences, differences in grape varieties, or differences in styles of wine.

Take geography first. Every wine writer will patiently explain that a classic Margaux will have more silkiness, more finesse than its equally fine Bordeaux brother, Paulliac, which produces wines that characteristically have more power and depth. But have you ever tried to verify this information yourself? If not, you might consider buying a chateau-bottled wine from each region—say a 1971 or 1974 (unless you have enough money to spring for two great wines from 1970).

In Burgundy, the red wines of the Côte de Nuits are generally considered to be more assertive than the lighter reds of the Côte de Beaune. Try a shipper's bottle from each area, again keeping the vintages the same: say, a 1972 Nuits-St.-Georges and a 1972 Volnay. Keep in mind that the purpose is not to see which wine is better but to determine the characteristics of each by comparing.

Other geographical matches could be 1976 Kabinett grade Rieslings from the Moselle and the Rhine—Piesporter versus Johannisberger—or a 1974 Cabernet Sauvignon from the Napa Valley with one from Sonoma.

Then there is the whole matter of California wines versus the corresponding "classic" European area. Try a good California Cabernet against a good red Bordeaux from Paulliac, Margaux, or St.-Julien. A Chenin Blanc with a Vouvray, also made from Chenin Blanc. A Sauvignon Blanc, also called Fumé Blanc, versus a white Graves or a Sancerre of Pouilly Fumé from the Loire; again, all have the same grape. Others would be a Johannisberg Riesling against a wine of similar sweetness from Germany, a Pinot Noir and a Burgundy, and a Chardonnay versus a white Burgundy.

As far as learning more precisely the differences in varieties of grapes whose differences may not be apparent to the beginner, try comparative bottles from the same California winemaker to avoid differences in wine-making styles. Experiment with a Krug Zinfandel against a Krug Cabernet, a Mondavi Fumé Blanc versus a Mondavi Chardonnay, and so on.

If you think all sweet, dessert wines are the same, try a Sauternes with a Moselle Auslese. What are the differences? Similarities? A lover of rosés should put his Mateus against Boordy's Rosé, his Tavel versus a Napa Valley Rosé of Cabernet Sauvignon, his Anjou against a Rosé of Pinot Noir.

Perhaps the most fertile sort of wine comparison deals with taste characteristics. Here, we use a bottle that has the characteristic against one which has none or little of it; the second bottle becomes the control.

For example, do you really know what a "flinty" taste is? If not, try a reputable 1976 Chablis (the real Chablis, of course) versus a white California jug wine. The Chablis will have a flat, metallic taste under the tongue—flintiness—while the jug wine will have none. Other characteristics, with the one that has it coming first: "foxiness"—Taylor's Lake Country White and Meredyth Seyval Blanc; "earthiness"—Hermitage Blanc versus a Moselle Riesling; "texture"—Meursault against Soave; "tannic"—a 1975 Médoc paired with red Chantefleur; "peppery"—Côtes du Rhone or Bardolino and a California Pinot Noir; "gaminess"—Chateau de Chaize from the Beaujolais versus a red Médoc; "oaky"—Calloway Fumé Blanc and a Mondavi Fumé Blanc. And so on. Read some of the descriptions in wine books first to better know what to look for.

Finally, the matter of vintages. In Bordeaux, 1972 was considered a vintage that made "thin" wines, while 1974 was a vintage that produced heartier, if not great, wines. Picking a secondary château, try one of each. Similarly, find out why the 1973 Cabernets tasted differently than the 1974s in California by trying one of each from, say, Louis Martini.

In wine, as in other matters, experience is the best teacher.

Chapter Six

Terms of tasting

SEVERAL weeks ago, I was sampling a sparkling wine from Penadés when I was struck by its unusual, yet pleasant, aroma which carried over into the taste. I was at a loss to describe it. Herbal? Perhaps, but "herbal" describes such a wide variety of smells and tastes. The nose did remind me of the brittle, pungent smell of the Arizona desert where I once lived. Yes, a bit like an ocotillo, I thought. Later, my wife was transferring some withered geraniums to the garage when a familiar odor came floating by. Eureka! Waving the Spanish wine bottle in one hand and a few crushed geranium leaves in the other, I confronted my wife (who is used to such displays) with my discovery. Yes, she admitted—the aromas of the geranium and the wine were the same.

The story may be a bit extreme, but it does prove a point: wine drinkers often go to some length to accurately describe a wine's taste and smell.

Why describe a wine at all? First, even many casual drinkers keep cellar logs or wine notebooks to jot down what they like—or dislike—about wines, not being content to trust sometimes faulty memories. Also wine writers, and those in the business, have the more difficult task of describing tastes and smells to a variety of readers with different backgrounds and experiences. Finally, those very enamored of wine, or who work in the trade, try to isolate a sensation and then try to account for it. Is, they ask, that "cooked" taste a result of oak casks or the ripeness of the berries? To most drinkers, however, this detective work is irrelevant.

While there are a few universal terms of tasting, most remain unscientific and personal. Some emotional pros even compare a wine to a symphony or an old mistress. The beauty of this is that even an amateur has the words to describe what he tastes, although it may take years of experience, and practice at concentration, to separate all the strands of a great wine to describe them in the first place.

The easiest and best descriptions are comparisons, some of which have almost become standards themselves. A fresh, dry Moselle Kabinett may taste of apples while a very sweet Moselle Auslese will remind one of the nectar of very ripe peaches. Chablis tastes of metal.

Powerful red Burgundies—the Roqueforts of wine—give off the pungent aroma of game meat. White Monterey wines often smell and taste like wet straw—pleasant, if not too concentrated. Light Rhône reds and Italian Bardolinos taste peppery, while stronger Rhônes may have a hint of creosote or road tar, which, in moderation, adds depth.

There are others: Red Bordeaux taste gravelly; white Graves can have a slight fishy taste; many wines in warm climates have the taste of earth; a very dry Champagne can have a sooty finish.

Sometimes you may want to stick to broader descriptions associated with taste buds: sweet, sour, bitter. Other commonly understood terms include dry, coarse, clean, hard, big, and fruity.

Of course, the French and others have their own terms that many experts use but which translate well into English.

Goût de terroir is another way of saying "earthy taste." Use the foreign terms if you like, but don't do it out of intimidation.

There are common terms for where or how wine strikes your senses—robe for color; nose for aroma; finish for the final taste at the top of your throat; aftertaste for what lingers. A complex wine will show different qualities or tastes as it passes the tip of your tongue, up over the top, around the sides of your tongue, and at the back. Hence, you may not only want to tell what you taste, or feel, but also where this occurs.

With a little practice, you can describe your wine to serve as a guide for further buying or simply to evoke memories. The notation "pale, platinum robe; spicy; apple-y nose; elusive taste—piquancy of a sharp, young Moselle with a subtle, sappy background of fresh oak and a light sparkling on the tip of the tongue," recalls to me, a particular California Chenin Blanc.

The challenge remains to find the exact words. One recent Mercurey I tasted had the odor of brown beans, slightly overcooked. Another Mercurey evoked an apt, although far from universal, description to my wife and me, both of whom grew up in the country where home canning was a prime summer activity. A few sniffs of the red Burgundy and we had the answer: "the smell of rubber sealing bands stuck to the glass liner of metal canning tops."

Somehow, I don't think that description will ever find its way into a standard text on how to identify the wines of Burgundy.

Chapter Seven

What detracts from tasting

NOT long ago, a friend and I were having lunch in a restaurant that likes to provide a changing variety of average-priced wines by the glass. She ordered a French Colombard and I took a Zinfandel.

After a couple of sips, we switched glasses to see if the wine really tastes better in the other glass. To my amazement, the lowly Colombard gave off a nice, flowery aroma unusual for such a wine. As we talked, I made a note in my book and then took a sip of the wine. Strange, its taste did not match the scent.

When she returned the Zinfandel, the mystery was cleared up. It now had the same aroma—not of the Colombard, but of her perfume, which lingered in the bowl of the glasses.

The phenomenon is common even among cocktail drinkers. Who has not had a scotch or bourbon scented at the rim of the glass with the flavor of olives or lemon that the bartender had carried over from making some gin or vodka concoction?

The point is that there are a lot of barriers that can come between us and the true taste of a wine. These barriers can sway our judgment and cause us to wonder what someone else saw or didn't see in the same wine, or what we saw in an earlier tasting of the same wine. Some of the barriers are obvious, and some are not.

Take the time of day, for example. Morning is our freshest period, not only for our palate, but for our minds. (A small glass of oak-aged, room-temperature Chardonnay can easily replace orange juice for breakfast; however, society frowns upon before-noon drinking as a sure sign of alcoholism.) As a result, more serious tastings occur before lunch. Our senses are easily dulled by a day's work, two or three meals, and previously-consumed alcohol.

Not only is the time of day important, so is the time of year. A professional taster or buyer may be able to sort out the seasons, but few of us can appreciate a hearty Hermitage on a hot, humid day. The same goes for a chilled, fruity Beaujolais sipped in front of the fireplace.

Next, you have to take the condition of your own body into consideration before you consider the body of the wine. One of life's frustrations is to develop a horrendous head cold or allergy shortly before a tasting of rare Clarets. Another common malady is acid indigestion, which makes it difficult to fully appreciate a crisp, astringent white, such as a Chablis or a Champagne. We can anticipate that, as soon as the throat closes, the acid will be flowing both ways.

And even that early morning tasting can be spoiled by lingering toothpaste or, worse, mouthwash. A good rinsing is almost obligatory, which is one reason I believe in serving water as well as wine with a meal.

Rinsing may also be necessary if you've eaten pungent food not too long before you try the wine. A blue-cheese dressing at lunch may still be lingering along the gum lines to attack any wine that comes along in an afternoon tasting. Too much alcohol can also dull the senses, both in the mouth and the brain, so a couple of cocktails before dinner may cause you to love a wine, on general principle, that your senses barely got to meet.

Dispensing with the failures of your body, we can proceed with the wine itself. First, temperature. White wines are generally chilled, of course, while reds are not, but there can be excesses. At a blind tasting recently, the taste of a fairly assertive Chardonnay was masked by the chilling. It was not until I had discarded most of the wine and was swirling only a few drops around the side of the glass that the pure Chardonnay smell started to rise up. Similarly, much of the taste of a good red Burgundy or Bordeaux can be lost if the "room temperature" is in the high 70s or 80s.

Breathing time is important as well. I won't repeat here the various traditional periods recommended for exposing a wine to air by decanting before it is tasted. Not even the experts are in agreement as to what is the best time to taste any wine—after ten minutes or two hours. But one thing is certain—a relatively young Zinfandel will be harsher, more assertive if you drink it as soon as you open the bottle than it will if you drink it after it has been decanted for a couple of hours.

Finally, there is the resting condition of the wine. Two identical bottles will taste differently if one has been quietly resting in your cellar for a few days while the other has been jostled around during the purchase, left for twenty minutes in a hot car, and then driven home where it is plunged into the refrigerator or left beside the range as dinner is cooking. Even a Dr. Pepper won't stand being shaken before you open it.

Don't forget the condition of the glass. Its shape will determine whether the bouquet is gathered or dissipated. Additionally, too much unrinsed detergent can almost kill a wine (ever wondered why your Champagne didn't bubble?), and lingering milk residue will dull the taste with its lactic acid.

Food? Bland items such as cheese or roast beef will best show a wine without showing it up. I don't even like cheese for a serious tasting; crackers will do. For pure enjoyment, you can obviously match the wine with food. A Chardonnay will taste better with a veal in light sauce than it will with a grilled steak.

There are some dishes, however, that will make any wine less pleasant. These are extreme foods—very spicy or pungent, very sweet, or very bitter. Anything with a lot of acid (salad dressing), spices (garlics, *jalapeño* peppers), or chocolate (even with a dessert wine, although there are exceptions) will likely cause you trouble.

Smokers will cause you trouble, particularly if you're a non-smoker. There are smokers whose palates I respect, but even they seem to be bothered by someone else's smoking. I hate to be at a restaurant where someone's activated charcoal smoke has nestled into the bowl of my wine glass, like fog in a valley, before the wine is poured. I have little sympathy for the condition, now or later, of their lungs.

Finally, there is the company. Wine can best be detailed and appreciated in the company of two or three other wine lovers who take time to study and comment upon it.

But most of all, to really get the most from a wine, you have to learn to concentrate. I generally will make notes on a wine before I take it to the table at a dinner party. While I may enjoy the wine as I'm eating and talking, I may not notice its subtleties, let alone remember them.

If I do forget or can't take notes, I try to save a little (which will be somewhat affected by the contact with oxygen) to give a final check the next morning when my head and palate are clear. Which proves two things: We're back to drinking in the morning yet again, and, with all these barriers, it's surprising that we ever agree with anyone's evaluation of a wine, including our own.

Chapter Eight

Wine and food: consider the sauce

THROUGHOUT the centuries, there have been a few core existential questions which have puzzled man. Why am I here? Is there life after death? What wine do I serve with the main course?

And we are all familiar with the tentative answers: namely, to pay taxes; yes and no; and white wines with white meats and red wines with red meats.

But is that all there is? In the case of the third question, no. We must consider the sauce.

If we were to look at cooking the way we look at construction, then each dish would consist of a substrate and a finish. In a few cases, such as grilled steak and normal fried chicken, there may be no substantial finish. The dish stands alone like rough wood or stone, and the wine is chosen entirely on the basis of the meat. In other cases, the meat is dominant, but has a sauce—like wood with a light stain. Here, both must be considered when choosing a wine. In some cases, the sauce almost completely dictates the taste, just as a heavy coat of paint obliterates the wood tone beneath. Here, the sauce will generally dictate the wine.

Actually, there are only a few primary bases for main dishes. At the light end are shellfish and fish, which generally take a white wine. Next come dishes that may be either light or heavy, depending on the sauce: chicken, pork, veal, lamb, and a nonmeat—pasta. Finally, there are the heavy meats that almost always dictate a red wine, i.e., beef and larger game, either four-legged or fowl.

There are two basic sauces—brown, which begins with a juice that has been browned, often with a thickener such as flour; and white, which has not been browned and often has cream. Ideally, a brown sauce will ask for a red wine, a white a white wine.

A white sauce can be used on practically any dish but beef and game, and a brown sauce can be used on practically any dish except fish and shellfish. Even here there are occasional exceptions. For example, *Béarnaise* sauce—a white sauce dominated by tarragon—can be used as a nondominating sauce for beef, especially rare beef.

What does all this mean in practice? Simply that with few exceptions seafood will take more delicate white wines, while beef and game will generally take hearty reds. The middle group—chicken, pork, veal, lamb, pasta—will take either white or red, depending on the sauce. If there is no sauce, then it is almost strictly personal preference.

Take chicken as a case in point. Without a sauce, I might prefer a Chenin Blanc with roasted breast and a sprightly Côtes-du-Rhóne with a breaded fried chicken leg. With a sauce, we have a range of possibilities. Chicken Cacciatore, featuring a green pepper and tomato sauce, needs an assertive but not heavy red, such as a Barbera. Chicken Kiev, heavy with butter and herbs, needs an assertive white, such as a medium-bodied Chardonnay in the lower Burgundy style. Chicken Tetrazinni with its creaminess calls for a full, even subtly sweet, white, such as a Vouvray or white Hermitage.

The same principle holds true in varying degrees with other meats in this category, as well as pasta.

Obviously, it becomes awkward to carry bulky notes in our pockets on food-wine pairings as we trot off to a restaurant. Gradually, it is necessary to develop a feel for what wine will go with what dish, relying on your memories of tastes.

First, is the meat white, red, or basically neutral? Then consider the sauce. A spicy one will need an assertive wine. A rich one will need a full wine. A delicate one will need a whispery wine. In the case of whites, that might mean a Gewürztraminer, Chardonnay, and a dry Riesling, respectively. Some sauces demand earthy wines; others might call for wines that are full and complex.

This "feel" for what goes with what may not come overnight, but it does come very naturally and is generally more accurate than any cheat sheet. A *Boeuf Bourguignon*, for example, will taste different in one restaurant than it does in another. (It is also often helpful to consult with the waiter on the method of preparation of a particular dish *before* ordering a wine.) Additionally, personal tastes and body chemistry must be taken into account.

After all, what is sauce for the goose may not be sauce for the gander—whether you're considering food or wine.

Chapter Nine

The changing rules of wines

IMAGINE the following set of circumstances:

• The most valued red wines in the connoisseur's cellar are the big reds of California—Cabernet Sauvignons and Zinfandels—long-lasting wines with high alcoholic content.

• Red Burgundies, with few exceptions, are not seriously considered by the American buyer as they are pale and short-lived.

• Red Bourdeaux is highly praised but is seldom cellared for any great length of time.

• Italian wines compose the bulk of most cellars, being the standard for everyday drinking as the wines of the Mâconnais, Beaujolais, and Rhône districts once were.

• The true American taste in white wines, which was always suspected of being a bit sweet, has come out of the closet as dessert wines become the high-priced rage.

Although Americans exist on change and fads, there are a lot of wine ideas we are reluctant to let go of and generally with reason. After all, the predominance of Burgundy and Bordeaux in the wine world has existed for at least a century, so are we to expect change now? Don't all wine texts say the same things?

Yet it is possible—and I emphasize possible—that we are in the midst of the most significant set of changes in vinification and the veneration of same since the early 1800s. The roots of these changes are in a large part economic, in some part social, and in an undefinable part personal.

In the 1700s, most wine was aged, stored, and shipped in wooden barrels as it had been for centuries. Virtually all wines were drunk within a year or two before they oxidized. Burgundies were in large part pink wines—rosés—and nothing else.

Then at the turn of the century, as the idea of using corks as stoppers was developed, bottles that looked like something other than open-mouthed carafes came into being. Since the late 1600s, it had been known that the new miracle material stripped from trees—cork—could keep wine from oxidizing if it was stashed tightly in glass bottles. A century of experimentation brought about an unknown concept: strong, raw red wine that was left to age in bottles for many years grew to be enjoyable and complex in a way the pink wines could never be.

In a short time, the cork-and-bottle revolution replaced the Côte de Beaune area as the source of the most prized wines of Burgundy and replaced it with the Côte de Nuits.

Bordeaux was another matter. For a long time its wines were weak—even Lafite was less than nine percent alcohol—so heavy Spanish wine and brandy were added to the barrels before they were shipped to England. Corks gradually changed that, too.

Even the Rhine wines were affected. "An old brown Hock (Rhine)" had been the standard in England. No more. Delicate, flowery whites—protected by cork—were discovered and treasured.

In the past 100 years, there have been few substantial challenges to the predominance of Burgundies, Bordeaux, and the German Rieslings, or to the way they are made. An exception was the stumbling of Sauternes—highly prized in the Victorian era—which almost went the way of ten-course meals.

Changes started to occur in the 1960s and accelerated in the 1970s. Many of these were economic, caused by you and me and thousands of other American drinkers. Wine became a status symbol . . . and we wanted it now. None of this waiting ten years in the cellar.

We also like our wine lighter—even the reds. The French accommodated us, just as they would modern tastes in food with the Nouvelle Cuisine. By the late 1960s, many, if not most, of the Bordeaux *châteaux* were making wines that would mature in five years instead of ten—a fact that many wine books have failed to consider in their cellaring recommendations.

Still Bordeaux kept up its standards. Burgundy did not. Its wines have become more common as they are gobbled up by the Swiss and the French, who have taken a bigger interest as their buying power has gone up. There have been no signs that the decline is being reversed.

As demand has increased, secondary French wines—the ones that made up the everyday cellar—have become overpriced, even allowing for inflation. Italy, with its acres and acres of vineyards, stepped in and suddenly became the front-runner in wine imported by Americans.

Then there is the personal element that has nothing to do with economics. Take, for instance, the California wine makers. In many ways, they have worked miracles in showing they can make as good as or better than whatever Europe can trot out. This is not chauvinism, and the litany of accomplishments need not be repeated.

Additionally, the Californians have started a couple of trends. One is that marvelously strong wines of more than 14 percent (which was once the case in Burgundy) are being made from Zinfandel and Cabernet that have long-term finesse as well. Possibility: These wines will become the standard for "big reds" throughout the cellars in the world.

Second, Californians have discovered late-picking of white grapes attacked by *botrytis cinera*, or noble rot. The resultant wines—like Sauternes and the German auslesen—are sweet and delicious without being cloying. Possibility: This fad may become a standard as we rediscover the dessert or white "sipping" wine.

One man's predictions may be another's balderdash. If you like the world order the way it is and want to keep it that way, raise a glass of Champagne to the past. Sparkling wine is one area where the tremors of change are not pounding.

Chapter Ten

Reasons behind the rules

IT is interesting to observe how different people react to rules and traditions. What some of us see as rich, orderly, time-honored practices are stupid, outmoded, stultifying restrictions to others.

The rules of wine are no less a passionate subject of argument than are the rules of government or the rules of society. Occasionally it is helpful to reexamine them.

Wine rules, like folk medicine and common law, generally have a practical history. They became rules because they met some need, even if this need wasn't always fully understood. However, that does not necessarily mean they are all practical or necessary today.

Take the most basic wine rule of all—"White wine with white meat; red wine with red meat." The practical basis is obvious. Red wines are strong and sturdy and will overpower a delicate fish or poultry dish. A dry white wine cannot stand up to rare steak. Since most people have an innate preference to white or red wines, we might wish it otherwise. Chemistry, however, will overrule sentiment in all but the most warped palate.

Yet, here we have the Blue Nun people urging Liebfraumilch *über alles,* and even the respected Robert Mondavi allows as how he might sip a little Chardonnay with his beef. What are we to make of that? Is the rule a-comin' tumblin' down? Yes and no.

The Blue Nun ploy is nothing more than an advertising gimmick which all but the most naive drinker realizes. Indeed, there are those who would question whether Blue Nun goes with anything, but, in all charity, it can accompany poultry and stronger fish adequately. As to red meat, even a Big Mac could successfully attack and overpower the Blue Nun.

Mondavi, on the other hand, is a winemaker and not an eccentric one. He realizes that Chardonnays are being vinified stronger these days, with added oak aging, more time with the skins, and so on. It is almost as if California winemakers, in keeping with the times, decided the "feminine" white wines should be liberated to raise a little hell. For instance, a David Bruce Chardonnay makes California jug reds look like a bunch of pansies.

The point is, it is not only the color ("red" meat, "red" wines) that is important; it is also the body. While I might not want to drink Chardonnay with steak, it is defensible from chemical and gastronomical standpoints.

A second area of "regulation" is the progression of wine with dinner. While there is no current controversy involved here, it might do well to look again at the reasons behind the rules. The progression is: white before red, dry before sweet, light before heavy, common before great, young before old. The first three sets dictate that the physically lighter wines come first so that their subtlety will not be lost. The last two sets argue that you save the best for last. One might quibble a bit here that too much common or young wine could dull the palate before we ever get to the great one. That is the reason that a really fine red wine is best enjoyed with a bit of cheese by itself rather than being fourth or fifth in a multi-course dinner.

A literalist could be confused when some of these sets of progression contradict each other. For example, a Sauternes (white) is an excellent dessert wine which follows a meat course wine such as Burgundy (red). Experience and tradition tell us the rule of dry before sweet, used here, over-rules the law of white before red. In a multicourse meal, you will be called upon to make similar rulings.

Another rule: "A good Bordeaux must be aged for at least 10 years." Although I relish the saying "To drink a Bordeaux in five years is like eating a baby," many of us are eating babies these days. Most French red wines are being made to mature much quicker than before, so drinking a good Bordeaux within five years is not at all unusual. There is also the matter of taste. The British, seldom accused of impatience, drink their claret (Bordeaux) with less age than the French or we Americans. Maybe it's the conditioning of Yorkshire pudding, but their palate seems to like a dose of tannin that has not completely been tamed. Here, I am an Anglophile.

There are other rules, but let us consider a final one: "Sturdy red wines must be aired (uncorked and perhaps decanted) for a half-hour to three hours before drinking." Alexis Bespaloff, winemaster of all trades, has been debunking this idea for some time in *New York* magazine. With lighter vinification in the French wineries, this is not totally surprising, but he reports even the Barolo people are recommending drinking upon opening. This has generally been my preference, but it seems to go against the worldwide preference for lightness (light beer, lighter wines, Nouvelle Cuisine), because wine is most assertive just after it has been opened.

Now, I must go open two bottles of Hermitage, drink from one as the other airs, and ponder this matter further.

Chapter Eleven

In praise of older whites

AT a recent tasting staged by wine merchant Robert Haas, the participants were presented with an engaging lineup of 1978 whites: a Pouilly Fumé, followed by a Chardonnay from Oregon, and three white Burgundies—a Meursault-Blagny, a Puligny-Montrachet, and a Corton-Charlemagne.

Enough to make any wine lover whimper, primarily in anticipation, but also with a degree of caution that Haas kept repeating as the three Burgundies were poured: "Of course, this wine is a bit young, but it will develop well with age."

Additionally, the Oregon Chardonnay (from the promising new Sokol Blosser winery) had not quite collected itself, either. Of the five, only the Pouilly Fumé—a pleasant, flowery wine—was ready for drinking.

To everyone's delight, this white segment of the tasting had been loaded with the noble Chardonnay (as opposed to one Sauvignon Blanc), but it still raised a pertinent question: Have we clutched too closely to our *tastevins* the old maxim

47

that white wines should be consumed early while they are fresh, say within two to three years of the vintage?

Whenever this question is usually raised, the standard response is to say the rule still holds and to note the exceptions—sweet wines (such as the sugary German Rhines and Moselles, French Sauternes, and rich Loire dessert wines), full wines (such as California Chardonnays and white Burgundies from the Côte d'Or), and sparkling wines (such as Champagnes). But I think it questionable whether those are the only exceptions. Indeed, it is debatable whether or not the exceptions are those white wines which do not age well.

Everyone agrees that we routinely lay down and bottle-age fine red table wines because they have a key preservative, tannin, which is gained by leaving the skins in contact with the juice during the early stages of fermentation. White wines seldom have the skin contact, so the theory is that we should drink them while they are fresh.

Another preservative is sugar, and, like wines with tannin, sweet wines can gain in complexity over the years, assuming that such other elements as fruit and acid are in sufficient balance. Acid provides structure for the wine. Otherwise, it has no edge to it in the mouth and is thus fat or flabby.

The presence of high alcohol, glycerols, and certain solids—that feeling of substance on the tongue—can also add to the aging and complexity of a wine.

Why age? Again, a wine can mature and gain complexity in the bottle if all its elements are in good balance. In theory, there is an economic factor as well. We are supposed to profit from buying a new wine at a reasonable price and have it aging in our cellar as the market value goes up to an outrageous price. Sometimes it works that way; sometimes not.

At any rate, red wines in general are being made to age more quickly these days, although there are some holdout winemakers in Europe and California. Now, it is not unusual for a Burgundy to be ready in four years, a Bordeaux in five, and for both to be at their peaks in ten. Again, there are some exceptions at the top.

This means, however, that many whites have similar aging potential and staying power. The 1976 Napa Chardonnays are just now reaching their peaks—as are many '76 Burgundies and '75 Bordeaux, both classic reds. Many '75 and '76 sweet Rhines and Moselles are still improving and will last for some time. With such similarities in longevity, is there any reason not to cellar these whites as we do the reds? No, and in fact many experts do. Still, I believe the traditional list of whites to cellar is too short.

Not long ago I had a ten-year old Cortese, an everyday Northern Italian white. It was not a "sympathy date" on my part. The earthiness of the wine had allowed a character and depth I am sure it did not have in its fresh, unformed youth.

Without trotting out a string of examples, I consider these white wines candidates for four to six, even ten years of bottle aging in good vintages: Sweet wines, "full" wines, sparkling wines, earthy wines, and wines with oak.

On the other hand, these wines would profit little from bottle aging: Very dry wines, low-alcohol wines, flinty wines, and flowery wines.

Earthy wines have a grain-like taste to them, the way that beers and whiskies do, and not the flowery finesse that most wine drinkers seek. This type of wine generally evolves from hot-weather grapes (Mediterranean, Central Valley), and many wineries in hot-weather areas now use cold fermentation in an attempt to bring up the freshness. Personally, I think a five-to-ten-year-old white Hermitage has more character than most of the spate of cold-fermentation wonders we are now seeing. Examples of these earthy whites are Riojas from Spain, Rhônes and Midi wines from France, and most Italians, including some Northern Italian Rieslings.

Oak also adds an element to aging wines, particularly Chardonnays. Sauvignon Blanc can profit from wood, and I like an old white Bordeaux, particularly a Graves, for this reason.

With sweet wines there should be sufficient acid or tartness around the edges or cellaring is worthless. Otherwise, put them away and let the cobwebs take over.

Sparkling wines? Everyone loves an older, vintage Champagne. The English, sometimes an odd lot, often like a sparkling wine even after the bubbles are gone.

On the other side of the cork, there are some wines that do not seem to improve in the bottle. We count among these Sauvignons Blancs or Fumés Blancs vinified in the flowery mode, dry Rieslings, and Vouvrays. Crisp wines such as Chablis, Cöteaux Champenois, and Muscadet also should be drunk young, as should low-alcohol whites from northern areas such as New York State and the upper Loire (Sancerre, Pouilly Fumé).

Let me suggest this. Buy a new wine (since 1977) and an older wine (before 1975) from two or three of the following: White Rioja, white Bordeaux, white Rhône, Cortese, white Mâcon, and any white grown in the Monterey Peninsula.

Compare. If you don't particularly care for the older wines, then our palates are different. Continue as you are. But if you like, possibly even prefer, the older wine then you can harvest a bounty of tastes, not to mention some bargains. Many old whites are amazingly inexpensive. And you can also save money in the long run by cellaring.

Perhaps you may even prove that the exception as to when to drink whites is really the rule.

PART THREE
Wine at Your Table

Chapter Twelve

Secrets of service

As with most social matters, the success of serving wine with dinner parties depends on a combination of common sense and your own sense of style.

Yet, because many people feel uncomfortable with some aspects of wine selection and service, they feel uncomfortable with the whole process. This is not necessarily an idle fear: while there are few rigid rules, it is easy to spot a gross failure.

Many meals fail because the menu is chosen with only one thing in mind—the food. The wine is chosen as an afterthought. Ideally, both should be planned together. If you have a very good bottle of properly aged Bordeaux in your cellar, or if you have just bought one, there is no reason that the main course should not be planned around it. Conversely, the same is true if your butcher offers you some great cuts of veal.

Even a fairly basic meal can be made special by abandoning the idea that you need just one bottle of good wine for an occasion. Although your budget may raise limitations, I would suggest a minimum of three wines if you're inviting guests for a serious dinner. That would be a lighter white wine with the first course, a full-bodied white or red for the main course, and a dessert wine for the ending. One or two more selections could easily be added without being—or appearing—ostentatious. As wine-food pairings have been discussed earlier, those particulars need not be gone over here.

Just as you would shop for food, so you should shop ahead (or consult your cellar log) for wine. Once you have decided on the kind of wine (color, body, and age) for each course, you must decide on the quality. It has always struck me odd that people who spend lavishly on food will often scrimp on wine. I admit to a prejudice against jug wine, but I also admit that the prejudice is well-founded. Few jug wines have character, and the wines you serve with a good meal should have character.

If in doubt, check with your wine merchant—baring your soul, menu, and budget.

As far as quantity is concerned, assume that most adults can (and will) easily consume a half bottle of wine per evening meal and may drink a full bottle over a two-hour period. In part, consumption will depend on the existence of, and length of, pre-dinner cocktails. To be safe, figure a glass of wine for the first course, two glasses to a half bottle as you dawdle over the main course, and a glass for dessert.

For those who have at least a modest cellar, you should also mentally choose backup wines should a bottle you open prove unacceptable.

The selection being complete, you can proceed with pre-dinner planning. With most white wines that means only chilling the wine an hour or two before it is to be brought out to the table. Most red wines are to be served at room temperature, but if you have a cellar or basement, keep the wine there, as it is better to err on the side of coolness.

An older wine that has sediment may be decanted,

although there is nothing wrong with pouring straight from the bottle with steady hand and eye keeping the dregs, or mud, from flowing out as you near the bottom. Of course, you may want to decant all of your wines—an unnecessary but personal preference matter—in which case you can do this well in advance of guests arriving.

Since you have taken time to plan, there is absolutely no need for a sweaty, dripping ice bucket at the table. Plan to place your bottle directly on the table in a simple wine coaster, unless you have decanted, in which case you need something to keep a dripping red or sweating white from ruining the finish of the table.

Airing? Again, personal preference. The vogue is not to let the wine breathe too long, and I generally go with that trend. However, I do open the bottles for tasting well in advance of the meal, and if a red seems a bit hard and closed, I'll leave the cork off for an hour.

Obviously, then, I do not open the bottle at the table. It's not considered bad form to take bottle and corkscrew in hand at the table, but there are many reasons not to. You cannot sample your wine in advance, give it air, substitute a bottle without letting food get cold, or not bore people with your cork-pulling and wine-tasting prowess if you uncork at the table. Sparkling wines are a different matter, as you don't want to flatten the bubbles by advance opening. Here, juggle the bottle as little as possible, tilt it away at 45 degrees, slowly twist the bottle and not the cork, and have a glass at the ready in case it overflows.

Whether you open the bottle in the kitchen (and sample it there) or at the table, make certain you clean the neck inside and out with a napkin to get rid of sediment and bits of cork.

Next come the glasses, which should be stemmed, have a fairly large bowl that curves inward, and be clear. If you are serving wine and water or more than one wine, consider having up to three glasses on the table at the right side of the plate. Anything more than that gets cluttered. The largest wine glass should be for red, and the smaller for white, and the glass that is to be used first should be toward the inside.

So much for glasses.

Ideally, you should serve the food before the wine, as the temperature of the food is more critical. If you already tasted the wine in the kitchen, there is no need to make a restaurant-style tasting ritual at the table. Simply begin pouring on the left, serving women first if it makes you (and them) more comfortable.

Pour no more than a half of a glass to allow the wine room to be swirled and aired. A third of a glass is even better, even though you'll have to interrupt your own dinner more often to pour. With a party of eight or more, you'll obviously need additional bottles around the table, or tables, for self-service.

Otherwise, pour throughout the meal as you see the need arise. When pouring, use a napkin at the neck unless you have a steady and practiced hand. To minimize dripping, pour decisively, stop smartly with a quick tilt of the bottle while making a quarter turn left and a sharp turn right.

Remove glasses that have been used as you remove plates that have been used. Don't be hesitant about bringing out a fresh round of glasses for dessert or for multiple courses.

All too fussy? Not really. The ritual is part of the enjoyment—as long as it makes common sense.

Chapter Thirteen

Letting wines breathe

OPENING a bottle of wine is a little like pulling a cork on a genie.

We may be fairly certain the wine is a good genie, but often we don't know what kind of a mood he's apt to be in after being cooped up for a few years. And how we handle that mood often dictates how much enjoyment we're going to obtain.

For example, some old wines have a mustiness, as though the dank earthiness of the cellar has seeped through the bottle. Some new wines have a chemical odor, a little like the fabled "morning breath" of the mouthwash commercials. Some fine wines, reaching the fragility of old age, have a haunting, elusive beauty that lingers only a moment like a butterfly and then flits away forever.

When we open a bottle of wine, in short, we give it air, and, for better or worse, it will never be the same as the oxygen begins to change the elements in the wine. There is a conventional wisdom—now being challenged—about how we are supposed to treat this initiation. A few of these simple rules state:

• A white table wine needs only a swirl in the glass to release its aromas. Anything more will start the wine on the road to premature deterioration.

• A simple red table wine, such as a California "burgundy" or a Côtes du Rhône, needs to have the cork pulled only a few minutes—say 15—before serving.

• A Bordeaux, Burgundy, and their California counterparts which are of normal drinking age—anywhere from five to ten years—need 30 minutes to two hours before serving.

• A huge red wine, such as a Barolo, late-picked Zinfandel, or Port, may need as much as a day to come to our senses.

• A very old red table wine needs to be approached gingerly and perhaps have no airing at all lest it start on its way to vinegar, the graveyard of wines.

Why do some wines need more air than others?

Essentially, it has to do with tannin, that bitter or dusty sensation you get under your tongue—tasting a bit like the inside of a pecan shell—when you drink fine red wines. Wines get tannin from grape skins, seeds (pips), stems, and wooden casks, the amount of tannin being determined largely by the type of grape and the desires of the winemaker. White wines are seldom fermented in the skins.

Tannin is the primary preservative in wine, giving it time to "ripen" and grow complex. However, somewhere in the aging process the tannin itself will become mellow. Thus airing a wine primarily allows us to lessen the impact of the tannin and bring the wine to its full complexity. White wines, simple reds, and old fine reds have little tannin or mellowed tannin, and hence need less air.

We may also want to let a wine breathe to get rid of chemical odors and mustiness.

How we do this breathing has been fairly cut and dried. We can pour wine in a decanter (particularly if it is a red wine that has thrown a natural sediment), which is a way of giving it more air space in the widened vessel as well as aerating it further in pouring. We can just pull the cork, which is traditional but which actually has little effect due to the small amount of surface exposed to air. Or we can aereate the wine by swirling it in our glass at the table.

So far, so good. But a couple of years ago the wine writer for *New York* magazine conducted a series of tastings with wine experts in which they were served a series of wines, both straight from the bottle and traditionally breathed, the identities being kept secret, of course. *Overwhelmingly, the experts preferred the wine that had not been extensively aired.*

A revolution in the making? Perhaps not.

Not long ago, I asked several California winemakers (including one who participated in the above-mentioned test) what they recommended and what they practiced. To a person, they stuck to the traditional views on letting wines breathe.

Robert Mondavi says he might "pull the cork about 20 minutes before serving" one of his Cabernets. "With a great big wine—not too old—I would decant and leave for two to three hours. With a delicate wine, perhaps 15 minutes would be enough, and I'd let it come along in the glass."

The others had similar timetables. Paul Draper, winemaker at Ridge, likes to open the bottle and pour off a glass to provide the wine more surface space. Walter Schug, winemaker at Joseph Phelps, warns that many good California wines may have an initial off-odor due to secondary or malolactic fermentation. This can be overcome by moderate airing.

But it is owner Joseph Phelps himself who probably puts the controversy in its proper perspective. "Occasionally, the wine itself will have a chemical problem that can be overcome by letting the wine breathe," he says. "Beyond that, the whole matter is relatively subjective."

Of course, much of wine judgment *is* subjective, but generally the wine experts agree on the ground rules of proper behavior, including airing wines. Why the division now?

I suspect it's an outgrowth of the "Texas" school of California wine enthusiasts, many very experienced and knowledgeable, who worship at the altar of bigness for bigness' sake. That altar is, of course, a new oak cask filled with a huge Zinfandel or Cabernet of more than 13 percent alcohol which was fermented with stems, skins, and pips.

These people relish the taste of tannin, so it is not at all unusual that they prefer the taste that flows from a freshly opened bottle. Most winemakers and traditionalists, on the other hand, prefer a wine to be more balanced.

Such differences of opinion are not unusual. Many Englishmen like an old Champagne that has lost its bubbles and becomes a graceful "still" wine. The French, of course, shudder at this practice.

Personally, I go pretty much with convention when serving guests at a meal. When drinking wine for its own sake, however, I like to try the wine as soon as the genie comes out of the bottle, then an hour or so later, and even the next day, if possible. Generally, each stage has its charms, whether they are tannic or mellow ones.

Try it for yourself. Take a recent (1976 or 1977) California Zinfandel, a 1970 or 1973 Burgundy, and a 1978 California Chenin Blanc, testing each on opening, 15 minutes later, two hours later, and the next day.

You'll probably soon discover the mood in which you want to meet your genies.

Chapter Fourteen

Reds that can be chilled

ONE of the reasons for the popularity of Beaujolais, particularly during the summer months, is that it is one red wine that everyone agrees should be served cool. A moderate amount of chilling brings out the best of these fresh, fruity wines from the East of France, and they serve as good thirst quenchers on a hot, humid day.

If you enjoy your reds a bit chilled—or don't have the benefit of an air conditioner and dehumidifier—there are a number of reds other than Beaujolais that you can safely stick in the refrigerator.

Of course, we've all been taught that red wines are generally best at room temperature—depending on what your room temperature is. If it's 80 degrees, then it's too warm. If it's 50 degrees, then both you and your wine need a blanket. Most red wines are at their best between 60° and 70°, but there are some exceptions.

These exceptions are primarily at the lower end of the scale and involve reds that fall into one of three categories:

(1) fresh and fruity, (2) very light-bodied, (3) poorly made or lacking in character.

As far as the latter category is concerned, this is the reason a red jug wine may taste better the second time around—after you've stuck it in the refrigerator—than it did immediately after you opened it. Chilling tends to hide minor defects in a red wine. Additionally, a blah wine tastes blah at room temperature, while it can at least quench your thirst when it is cool. I suspect this is the reason so many home winemakers routinely chill their reds.

As far as body is concerned, a Barolo or Hermitage would get muscle cramps in the ice box, but a light-bodied red actually becomes more spirited. If the whole matter of relation between body and temperature seems elusive, think of the lighter reds as being only one step away from a rosé, which is only one step away from being a white. Generally speaking, the lighter the body, the more that chilling brings out the character of the wine.

On the other hand, chilling helps bridle a fresh, fruity wine and makes it more palatable. Who wants to drink a warm cherry soda? The analogy isn't perfect, but you get the idea. Some fruity wines will develop an agreeable tangy or sour taste with a few years' age, and, for that reason, I occasionally enjoy a five-year-old Beaujolais at room temperature. It has developed a different character, and it needs no chilling because the fruitiness is gone.

With all this in mind, it is easy to think of a dozen or so wines that can benefit from a half-hour's chilling for summer drinking.

Beginning with the American wines, most jug wines, and Napa Gamays from California, are obvious cool-drinking candidates. In spite of their poor reputation—which is generally deserved—some of the "foxy" New York wines can present an economical change of pace. The blends served up under such labels as Lake Country Red can be refreshing, very fruity picnic wines.

For a change of pace, a slightly peppery Côtes-du-Rhône can be a cooling companion to grilled hamburgers and goes about as well with raw onions as anything can. Also from France, a light Chinon from the Loire Valley can be chilled. Not all Chinons are light, however, although most are, due to the northern growing season.

Some of the better bargains in light wines come from Italy. Two especially come to mind, although many people have difficulty in distinguishing between them—Valpolicella and Bardolino. The confusion is not unwarranted. Both come from the same grape variety, although soil conditions are different.

Also from Italy are the ubiquitous Lambruscos from near Bologna. It is not an oversimplification to refer to these as "beginner's wines," as far as Americans are concerned, because new drinkers are drawn to their soda-pop fruitiness and fizziness. If they are to be drunk at all, it is when chilled.

From Spain, inexpensive Rioja claretes can be iced, as can the very light but alcoholic Valdepeñas, the cafe wine of Madrid. This is my favorite light, hot-weather red, but it is almost impossible to find in American stores.

Of course, there are some traditionalists who will have none of this chilling of red wines, and I admit that, for myself, I prefer most reds warm regardless of the season. However, with the types of wines we're talking about, few could argue that there will be any great taste loss one way or another.

Let's just leave it as a private matter between you and your Kelvinator.

Chapter Fifteen

Serving a wine with every course

Too often people in the United States—and Europe, as well—think of a meal with more than one wine as a thing of the past, something that went out with Hudson pouring for the Bellamys upstairs as Mrs. Bridges whipped up another course downstairs. Yet an extra wine or two can add much to an evening with so little effort. Serve a light white with an appetizer course, perhaps a bold Burgundy or Rhône with cheese before dessert, or a sweet wine with—or instead of—dessert.

There are a few rules to follow and to break, the same rules you observe at a wine tasting: white before red, light before heavy, dry before sweet, young before old, common before regal.

Appropriately, consider first the appetizer course. The wine, like the food, should whet the appetite. It will probably be white, light, fresh, young, and the most common of the evening's wines. It might be a simple Muscadet or a Mâcon blanc or a Soave, Riesling, Frascati, or Pouilly Fumé.

A serving of a light pâté with a couple of sweet gherkins

or cornichons on the side might call for the Mâcon blanc, a white Graves, or a dry Riesling.

A slice of quiche Lorraine could use an Alsatian Riesling or Sylvaner or even a Muscadet.

Light pastas with thinner cream sauces are becoming more popular as appetizers (presuming pasta is not the main course), and a medium-bodied Italian white such as Orvieto would be a welcome accompaniment.

Shellfish prepared simply would do well with either a Muscadet or a Chablis. Escargots can take either a red or white, but the wines should be of some substance and not at all light. *Crudités* go well with medium reds such as Bardolino, Zinfandel, Côtes-du-Rhône.

Then comes the part of the meal with which we are most comfortable using wines—the main course—and there is no need to repeat what has already been discussed about wine and food pairings at this point. Obviously a meal should be planned as a unit, though, so the main course and the wine that goes with it determines the appropriateness of the earlier and latter courses, as has been noted with appetizers.

The contents of the main course may also determine whether or not you would insert a cheese course between it and dessert.

A partially ripened Camembert or one of the blue-veined cheeses can take a strong Burgundy, Hermitage, Côte Rôtie, or Barolo. Slightly milder cheeses would be in good company with a California Cabernet Sauvignon, a lighter Burgundy, or a fine Bordeaux.

The final possibility for adding a wine to your meal is with dessert. Many people swear they don't like sweet wines— and with good reason, considering the sticky whites that were once the mainstream of California—but perhaps they will enjoy dessert wines if they try them. Give them a chance.

Most dessert wines are white, so this is where we may violate that white-before-red rule. A more substantial issue is how and when to drink your wine—with dessert, after dessert, or instead of dessert. Many wine writers opt for the latter two, but I'm with the minority who enjoy a sip of wine while munching on meal's end.

Essentially, there are two types of dessert wines. One is the sweet, red, fortified wines such as Port, cream sherries, and some Madeiras, generally, although by no means always, taken away from the table. These are more familiar to most of us.

The other class is the sweet, generally unfortified whites that get their richness by having been allowed to linger on the vine while a fungus *(botrytis cinerea)* draws off water and leaves sugar. Within this category are wines of considerably different tastes—Sauternes from France, Riesling and Sylvaner Auslesen, Beerenauslesen, and Trockenbeerenauslesen from Germany (and their counterparts beginning to get a fungus-hold in California), Tokaji Aszu from Hungary, and the 57 (or 157) varieties of Muscat wines from California and the world (some of which are red). They should all be served cold.

A lovely way to be introduced to Sauternes is to have a quarter of a glass served with a slice of pound cake. (Always pour a modest amount of these heavy dessert wines.) Some Sauternes hint of the piquancy of a sherry without the nutty flavor or even a Madeira, while others have overtones of light honey. They are all thick and luscious.

Chateau d'Yquem, the queen of Sauternes, costs well up into the double bills when you can find it. Outrageous? Not when you consider that the grapes may be picked over five to ten times by harvesters taking only a few fully botrysized berries at a time, while the owner prays that the rains will hold off and not ruin his crop. Anyway, you can get a pleasant shipper's wine from good years such as 1969, 1970, or 1971 for $4 to $6. Moderate age of at least five years will improve most sweet wines.

Tokaji Aszu has a darker taste which hints of molasses,

but don't be put off by the comparison. It is neither over-sweet nor overthick. It goes well by itself, with a neutral dessert or with one that has been lightly flavored with caramel (such as flan), or with pecans.

Tokaji Aszu costs about $6 for a small bottle in its richest form—"five *puttonyos*"—which is prominent on its label. Don't try to comparison shop on brands—it's all marketed by the Hungarian government.

Sauternes is my favorite wine with dessert, but the Ausleses (or Auslesen) from the Rhine and the Moselle are my favorites as dessert, either at or away from the table. German wines with few exceptions carry the village, vineyard, and vintage in large type (Piesporter Michelsberg 1976er, for example) with the degree of initial sweetness just under this. Kabinett is the basic level with the lowest sugar. Next is Spätlese, followed by Auslese, which generally start at around $4 to $5 for lesser vineyards. These can be quite good. (Remember that wines labeled "trocken" are *always* dry.)

There is only one word to describe a good Auslese, and that is "nectar," for it tastes at its best like a very elegant peach or apricot.

There are even sweeter German wines, of course—the Beerenauslesen and Trockenbeerenauslesen. The latter are extremely difficult to find, and the former are somewhat rare, although the richness of the 1976 vintage has provided more of them than usual on the shelves. A simple Beerenauslese generally costs more than $15, even if it is the secondary Sylvaner grape rather than the traditional Riesling. Still, even an "inferior" Beerenauslese is a princely wine.

The Muscat wines from California are not really to my liking. They all have a distinctive creamed raspberry taste that isn't as pleasant as it sounds. Muscats have been blended into the so-called "Rhines" of many brands over the years—those very same sweet wines we've loved to hate. ·

If you want to try for yourself, Christian Brothers makes

a light, Muscat-flavored wine called Chateau La Salle and Beringer bottles a thicker one called Malvasia Bianca. Both are inexpensive.

It might be too much of a switch to go from one to four wines in one meal, so you may want to experiment with the main course and dessert. I prefer a three-wine meal for a special occasion or a weekend dinner with guests—appetizer, main course, and dessert.

On Monday, however, the normal routine returns: a one-course meal of grilled hamburgers with sliced onions and a $2 bottle of Côtes-du-Rhône.

Somewhere, Hudson weeps.

Chapter Sixteen

Classic wines for classic dishes

THE next time you trip out to by freshly made *pâté de foie gras* (or decide to whip up a batch in your Cuisinart), try something different—not with your recipe, but with the wine you serve with it. Normally, most of us would try to cut the richness of the goose liver with a brut Champagne, the acidy bubbles teasing our jaded palate back to life.

Next time, serve a 1970 Sauternes instead. Of course, you may decide to skip the fish course, the meat course, and the dessert, as the calories roll down and the desire to go nodding off in the sitting room takes over.

Foie gras and Sauternes—a match of "likes" rather than a match of contrasts (as is the case with *foie gras* and Champagne)—is not for everyone. But it is the traditional pairing, a carry-over in part from the Victorian days with their long, heavy meals. And, under the right circumstances—say a late evening snack—it still works out very well.

(Parenthetically, wine expert Alexis Lichine has only one reservation concerning Americans who want to observe the custom. "Regrettably, good *foie gras* is not easily available outside of France," he sniffs.)

Traditional matches of food and wine—such as these—are interesting exercises for anyone who enjoys experimenting at the table. Some of these pairings are logical ones, which trial and error have molded over the years, a long-term experimentation in food chemistry, as it were. Other pairings, such as the Sauternes and goose livers, are reflections of life styles, as food and drink generally become when one gets beyond the subsistence level. Most traditional matches are regional pairings, logical extensions of drinking and eating what is at hand, even if the combination did—and does—leave a bit to be desired. Finally, some pairings are a result of "saucing"—pouring into the glass the same wine that you have just added to your sauce in cooking.

Probably the most famous of these wine and food matches is caviar and Champagne. Not only is it a good pairing in principle, it also reflects the ethics of elegance. Rare, expensive food matched with rare, expensive wine.

Less rare, but equally traditional, are oysters and Chablis. Of course, we are talking about the real Chablis that comes from the same region in northern France, and not the California generic bastardization. As is the case with most shellfish, the crisp, dry, metallic Chablis serves as the perfect complement to the delicate morsels.

Moving up the menu in "heaviness," we come to the traditional matching of sole and white Burgundy. Of course, the sauce—here as always—is important in determining what type of wine to serve with the dish. For example, a good white Burgundy would go very well with a sole poached in a white wine sauce, but would be a disaster with curried sole, sole with Bordelaise sauce, or sole with tomato sauce.

Moving from fish to red meats, lamb with Bordeaux—particularly a Saint-Emilion—is a matchup straight from the cookbooks. Beef can go with a number of red wines. But it is not surprising that beef with a Bordelaise sauce is traditionally accompanied by a Bordeaux, typically a Médoc, while *boeuf Bourguignon* is at home with a fine Burgundy from the

Côte de Nuits. This coupling, of course, is a matter in large measure of saucing.

Burgundy has also long been the wine of large game, and a cut from a leg of venison and a Côte de Nuits, perhaps a Chambertin or a Nuits-St.-Georges, is de rigueur.

Such regional potluck dishes as Hungarian goulash go with the best local wine, in this case Egri Bikavér or "bull's blood." The cassoulet of Languedoc—a bean casserole with pork, lamb, or fowl—traditionally takes a regional red wine such as Minervois, Fitou, or Corbières.

Some regional pairings may seem a bit odd at first. Sauerkraut dishes, for example, would not seem to go with any wine, beer seeming the better companion. Yet the Alsatian dishes of sauerkraut or *choucroute*, which have sauces and meats, can be matched rather comfortably with Alsatian Gewürztraminer, the spiciness of the wine standing up to the fermented cabbage.

Moussaka, with its eggplant and lamb, may give you the one opportunity in your life to have an excuse to drink Retsina, the resin wine of Greece that makes us wonder about the palate of Dionysius.

Less controversial is the delightful Swiss pairing of cheese fondue—or of raclette—and Neuchâtel or a related white Swiss wine. Of course, meat fondue calls for entirely different wines.

To end the meal, have a nibble of the richly veined English blue cheese, Stilton, and a vintage Port, a combination that has sustained the English for years. Or, if Stilton isn't your preference in ending anything, have the equally traditional ripe peach half with a glass of sweet, luscious Sauternes on the side.

However, if it is the same Sauternes with which you began the meal back there with the *pâté de foie gras*, then you will definitely need to retire to the sitting room for a comfortable nap, unbuttoning the top of your trousers as any true English gentleman would do.

Chapter Seventeen

When game is the name

IN my hillbilly'd youth in West Virginia, I enjoyed tromping through the night woods as the dogs bayed in the distance trying to tree a 'coon or 'possum. Once or twice I even picked up a 22-caliber rifle to go hunting with some of my high school buddies, which caused them amusement as one has to be a better shot than I was to bag a squirrel with anything less than a shotgun.

The truth was, of course, that I was along more for the lark than the squirrel. But in growing up in the country I did acquire a love for game meat—even if I didn't want to be the one to shoot it.

I still have relatives back there who are avid hunters and who could have played as extras in *Deliverance*, although I might hesitate to make that observation if one of them had a 12-gauge in his hands at the time. Come winter, they help me fill up my ice chest with venison and rabbit on my trips back to Aaron's Fork.

Unfortunately, many wine lovers never get to make the pairings of wine and game, either because they don't have access to game or else don't know how to prepare it. It is worth the trouble to find the meat and the method.

Wild game, by its nature, is more pungent and assertive than its barnyard and feedlot counterparts, and this gives us an opportunity to make the most of some of our more assertive red and white wines.

For four-legged game, whether deer or rabbit, few wines can match the pungency—in truth, gaminess—of the meat than can a California Pinot Noir or its counterpart, a red Burgundy. There is a simple rule of thumb as to which wine to use within this range: The larger the game, the more assertive the wine.

Two personal examples can illustrate the point.

My wife is a master (mistress?) at preparing game, and one of the best game meals I have had centered around a young wild rabbit. The traditional country way for "taming" the gaminess of meat is to soak it for a day or so in the refrigerator in a light salt brine. Generally, it is then rinsed and cooked. Like the Europeans, however, Ella takes the process a step further by marinating the rinsed meat for a couple of more days in a good, yet lesser, wine.

In this case, our rabbit was marinated in a Bourgogne Passe-Tout-Grains, a red blended wine, and then cooked lightly and served simply with beans and potatoes. The accompanying wine was a light 1973 Chambolle-Musigny, making a perfect match and a delicious meal.

Another time Ella prepared a venison steak in the same manner, but it was paired with a stronger 1970 La Romanée. Again, a superb match and meal.

Among California Pinot Noirs to use with game, my preferences tend to go in two opposite directions, either choosing an older Pinot Noir that has begun the first stages of browning, or deterioration, or else a young, flashy Pinot such as those made by Davis Bynum. The selection of these opposites is not as strange as it might seem. An old Pinot

73

brings out the woodsy, earthy elements of the grape, while the young Pinot emphasizes the rich pungency.

Cabernets, either in California or Bordeaux, are not earthy or pungent enough to make ideal companions to my way of thinking for game, but there are good possibilities other than Pinot Noirs.

Mediterranean wines in general go well with wild fare. For heavier meat such as deer, try Côte Rôtie and Hermitage from the Rhône and Barolo and Amarone from Italy. Rabbits can take a better Beaujolais such as a four- or five-year-old Morgon, a Châteauneuf-du-Pape, or a Chianti.

Depending on the age of the animal, type of animal, and preparation, wild fowl can take either a red or white wine. Often it is strictly a matter of personal preference.

For a Thanksgiving dinner a few years ago, some friends roasted a wild goose using an Alsatian-style stuffing of raisins and sauerkraut. We were to bring the wine. Since a goose is almost of red-meat intensity, we knew that traditionally a red wine is served with it. Still, we did not dismiss the whites. Taking the diplomatic way out, we showed up with a Hermitage and an Alsatian Gewürztraminer.

Two glasses were set for each person—and the Gewürz won legs down as the best match, although the Hermitage was very much in the ball park. In this case, a very assertive and spicy white wine did a better job of standing up to the fat and pungency of the goose. Not to mention the sauerkraut.

For lesser game birds, such as quail or pheasant, a larger white will probably do as well as traditional reds. An oak-aged California Chardonnay would be very good, as would one of the Côte d'Or Burgundies, such as a lesser Montrachet or a Meursault. This is assuming that the bird is roasted and prepared fairly simply. As has been discussed elsewhere, sauce and preparation are often the determining factors as to what wine to serve—even more than the meat in many cases.

If you have your appetite whetted for a game meal, there are several options to follow. The easiest is to find a restaurant that regularly serves game. Pheasant is fairly universal, but getting venison might take a bit more searching. Anyway, once you've found the restaurant, you can only pray the wine list has the appropriate bottles.

A second route is to check with your butcher for the availability of game. If he doesn't have it, he can probably tell you where to find it. Many hunters are like my relatives in that the chase is more important than the prize, which they sell. Once you have the game in hand, it is easy to find a cookbook that can give you specific directions on preparation—although the brine and wine soakings are recommended as a start.

Or you might decide to go hunting yourself. If you're no better at it than I am, set aside a few bottles of a recent vintage of Burgundy. By the time you make the kill, the wine should be well-aged.

Chapter Eighteen

Wines that go with ham

HAM is the traditional main dish for an Easter feast—as turkey is to Thanksgiving and goose is to Christmas—but what wine do we drink with it?

While planning the Easter menu, we might think, ah yes, a chilled Vouvray will be just fine. Later on, the mind might wander to a light red, such as a Beaujolais, or a Bardolino; even a Médoc might seem in order.

Someone mentions a rosé. Not a bad idea, we admit.

Or, if we want to be particularly festive, how about a sparkling wine from Champagne or the Napa Valley? Or even a sparkling Vouvray?

To paraphrase a cliché, ham goes with everything—and nothing. That is, it comes very close to being a neutral entity as far as wine goes, so much so that some experts throw up their hands and recommend beer. As much as I love beer, I would not be that drastic, except perhaps with a ham sandwich or a ham sub.

Part of the problem with ham is that it is a red meat with many of the characteristics of white meats. It is light in texture, color, strength. It has a high fat content, as we cholesterol counters will recognize. By use of sauces and other accompaniments, it can be made sweet or tart, heavy or light.

Because of these characteristics, ham spans the range of wines from full whites to light reds. However, it is much too substantial for light whites, such as Chablis and Muscadet, and too light for heavier reds, such as Côte d'Or Burgundies, assertive Cabernets Sauvignons, Hermitages, Barolos, and so on.

Additionally, what ham needs is a wine with acid as well as a moderate body. Acid is needed in any wine that accompanies a dish with fairly high fat content.

For that reason, a sparkling wine often is served with basic roast ham. It is true that many sparkling wines, including Champagne, fall into the category of lighter whites, but the reason they stand up to ham, where most lighter table wines would not, is their acid content. This acid comes in part from the bubbles—the carbonation—so that the combination of acid and the fizziness work particularly well.

Similarly, unadorned roast ham can take on a variety of white and red partners. Vouvray, with its full body and touch of sweetness, can go particularly well. So can a full-bodied Chardonnay, such as those made in California and the Côte d'Or of Burgundy. (Chablis is also made from Chardonnay, but it is too dry and fragile for pork.) A full-bodied Fumé Blanc would also be a fitting drink for your Easter meal.

Rosé—the bastard-child wine that most serious drinkers ignore—is a natural for ham, as it by definition embodies both the characteristics of red and white that meat demands. Pass up the Portuguese and French wines for a change and try a Maryland or Virginia rosé (I particularly like Boordy's), a California rosé of Pinot Noir, or even the Greek Rodytis.

If you prefer reds to whites as a rule, then look for such light to medium reds as the Italian Bardolinos or Valpolicellas, Côtes-du-Rhônes, Beaujolais, everyday Médocs, a Rioja clarete from Spain, or a lighter Zinfandel from California. All of these have sufficient acid to stand up to the ham, but not too much body to overcome it. Incidentally, many California red jug wines lack this acid, so don't be tempted.

What if your ham is not going to be your everyday, run-of-the-mill roasted variety?

The same rule for sauces applies to ham as for any other dishes. If your ham, or a primary side dish, is to have some variant of a brown sauce, serve a red wine. Similarly, a white sauce and its variants will take a white wine.

More popular than using either white or brown sauce is the practice of making ham sweeter or saltier. Both practices do damage to wine (hence the cry for beer), but neither are fatal.

For instance, don't buy a great wine to go with your unsoaked or lightly soaked Smithfield. However, if you like a certain tanginess to your meat, a red will cope with it better than a white. I probably would use a recent Côtes-du-Rhône.

Unusual sweetness can be matched by a Vouvray or a fruity red, such as a Beaujolais, either served quite chilled. A sparkling wine of less than brut dryness can also be used.

A spicy ham also causes problems, and the Gewürztraminer from Alsace or California is probably your best ally against cloves and similar spices. A heavy mustard sauce spoils the palate for any wine, but a very acid red, such as an everyday Chianti, might be of some help.

If you really love ham—and really love wine—you might be tempted to have two or more bottles available on the sideboard to test your own preference. After all, since you can't justify a great, expensive wine with ham, why not a couple of good, inexpensive ones?

Chapter Nineteen

What to serve with oriental food

"**T**HE concept was that there was an opportunity to sell wine in Chinese restaurants," Peter Stern recalls in the tasting room at Turgeon & Lohr in San José. "So I set about designing a wine to go with Chinese food."

A formidable task, but then Stern is the successful winemaker at Turgeon and a graduate of the product development group at Gallo. Of course, some very nice wines have come from Gallo's product development, but then so has Boone's Farm.

Anyway, Stern set to work on finding the proper blend and arrived at a wine that was a little sweet and slightly spicy—part Johannisberg Riesling (60 percent), part Sylvaner (25 percent), and part Gewürztraminer (15 percent).

It was given the name "Jade," and it quickly became a successful part of the company's J. Lohr line of wines. Later, the composition of Jade was changed to respect the high price of Riesling grapes. Stern has substituted Burger, a nondescript workhorse grape that he calls "light and fruity if cold fermented," although Riesling remains (20 percent) as does Gewürztraminer (20 percent).

My own tasting notes of a few months ago describe Jade, in part, as "a bit heavy and moderately sweet, but with a clean finish. Hints of Sylvaner Spätlese, although more like a Vouvray."

But does it go with Chinese food?

Let us consider first a more general answer from Howard Hillman's *The Diner's Guide to Food*. He writes: "I frequently read articles and hear amateur epicures of the Western world attempting to delineate which wine makes the ideal accompaniment to Chinese cuisine. Personally speaking as an experienced Chinese cook and diner, I think their efforts are an exercise in futility. They should be addressing themselves to 'whether' rather than 'which' wine will marry well with Chinese food. And the answer to the 'whether' question is 'no' for a variety of reasons."

Most wine writers go along with Hillman, although in a pinch they cite possible choices from fullish whites to non-fullish whites, also for varying reasons. And most believe that Gewürztraminer is the best possibility of all—so maybe Peter Stern is on the right track.

There are essentially two reasons why Oriental foods give us wine drinkers, who hate to face a plate without a wine glass, such difficulty. One is that they can have so many ingredients that tend to overwhelm wine—sweet sauces and hot spices being two of the primary ones.

A second reason for the lack of harmony is that, unlike Western cuisine, Eastern cookery grew up without the influence of wine made from grapes. Oh, China has grown wine grapes for years, but little wine has resulted from it. And Japan, with its wet climate which harbors diseases of the vine, has only begun cultivation in the past few decades.

It is true that some of you might have seen something named "Wan Fu" on your wine merchants' shelves or on the wine menu at a Chinese restaurant. Wan Fu is an interesting and fairly decent white wine that seems to blend the fruitiness of a Vouvray and the crisp finish of a Muscadet, both Loire wines. The French resemblance is not incidental, as this Oriental wine is made in France. The green bottle that sits before me has a pastoral Oriental scene (as perhaps interpreted by the Brandywine school) and several Oriental symbols in red. I do not know what they mean, but perhaps Sichel, which bottles and ships Wan Fu, may one day explain.

Without having to worry about reds, whites, and rosés Oriental drinkers have contented themselves with wines made from rice. Japanese Sake is the most readily available form for American drinkers. Sake is technically a beer, but the American government considers it a wine, and it tastes something like a grape wine. Traditionally, it is served warmed in small ceramic vessels, but it can be drunk at room temperature at the table with food. It tastes slightly sweet and spicy with a clean finish.

Although I like Sake, it does not strike me as a particularly good partner with food (I prefer it before a meal), although many writers, routinely recommend it as it is Oriental. (Perhaps Chinese writers think that Dr. Pepper is what all Americans drink with steak and fried chicken.) My own kneejerk reaction is to order green tea, even if it doesn't have alcohol.

Does that mean that Jade and Wan Fu are gauche and that all wines should be banned from the Chinese table? No, Howard Hillman to the contrary. While it is true that many Oriental foods do not complement wine, and while it is also true that most Chinese restaurants understandably have subpar wine lists, there are still a number of dishes that can be enjoyed with wine.

The key, as always, is not to memorize matchups, but to match your own remembered tastes. For example—a lightly seasoned rice with beef. Considering the taste, my memory would suggest a slightly "peppery," medium-bodied red—a Côtes-du-Rhône or lesser Rioja. A similar dish with chicken—perhaps a white Hermitage.

My line of reasoning in choosing wines for Oriental dishes goes like this: A sweet sauce or hot spices automatically reject the possibility of a wine. Those two not being present, I would choose a red or a white wine depending on the type of meat. As the meat portion is normally subdued, I would go for crisper whites and medium to light reds, most rosés being too sweet. A vegetable dish would generally work better with a white wine. If a white wine dish is slightly spicy, pair it with a Gewürztraminer. Heavy on the soy sauce, lean toward a red, although an overdose of soy can kill any wine.

This group of generalities—which has served me well with Japanese, Korean, and Chinese dishes—seems about as far as you would want to go in making recommendations as to whether, or what, to drink with Oriental foods.

So don't hesitate to try Sichel's Wan Fu or J. Lohr's Jade, although neither will go with all Oriental food anymore than Blue Nun goes with both Stiller and Meara.

But just to set the record straight, a final word from Peter Stern: "Actually," he confesses, "I don't drink Jade in Chinese restaurants. I want beer with Chinese food."

Chapter Twenty

The daze of wine and salad

A green salad. Small thing, really, but such a nuisance What to do with it when it comes to drinking wine with a meal?

Of course, you could ignore it completely. Take a bite of rare steak, a forkful of lettuce, tomato, and celery with a drizzle of Italian dressing, then a sip of 1970 Paulliac. Pretend not to notice.

But, dash it, there it is, that salad messing up a perfectly good wine, throwing it slightly off balance with its acidity.

Worse yet, what about when you want to make a meal of chef's salad and still have wine to drink? A decision of agony.

It's not the salad, actually. Most vegetables are rather neutral with wine. They more or less coexist, like a lap cat and a shin-rubbing dog. It's the dressing that's the villain. Most dressings—Italian, Russian, whatever—have vinegar, and vinegar is to wine what Dillinger was to Hoover—Public Enemy No. 1.

And it's not the only enemy. Howard Hillman, again, in

83

his *The Diner's Guide to Wines* has an enemies list that would make the White House proud.

For example, would you be so thoughtless as to expose your wine to cranberries? What about molasses? They're both antagonistic to wine. Hillman also condemns hot stuff (chili, curry, tabasco, mustard, horseradish), egg yolks, chocolate, artichokes, asparagus, onions, oily fishes (such as tuna), candied vegetables, and citrus fruits—villains, all.

Actually, I agree with Hillman in most instances. I might drink a Barbera with spaghetti and tomato sauce, but I can feel the battle raging all the way down to my stomach. Pickles? Yes, they're bad, but who would forgo cornichons with pâté and wine? I don't eat bananas, but they would seem to be without guile. And I can take chocolate in some forms with a dessert wine, say, a frothy mousse.

Hillman is wise in recognizing that not all enemies are equal: "Some, like vinegar and chocolate, can be vicious villains, while others, such as artichokes and asparagus, are not quite so hostile."

But we digress. The salad, present at almost every meal, must be dealt with.

If I'm not having an appetizer served at the table when I'm entertaining, I may begin the meal with a salad but serve no wine until the plates are cleared. Water can clear the palate, and we can go on to substantial food. Or, on occasion, the Continental style of serving the salad somewhere between the main course and the dessert course can be handled in the same manner. If you like to fuss a bit in the kitchen, a sorbet, the French sherbet-like ice, can be used to clear the palate, no matter where you stick the salad.

But what if you like your salad *with* the main course, or if you don't want to juggle glasses to accommodate it? Well, you could have salad *au naturel*, figuring there is enough taste in the vegetables alone without a dressing. But let's face it— raw vegetables are like so much filler to most people, hence the dressing to make it palatable.

There are options, however, with what you can put on a salad to give it that flavor. Mayonnaise may have vinegar, but not enough to do the damage that a vinegar or garlic dressing would. Even better is plain yogurt. Or sour cream.

Another route is oil without vinegar. Or some bacon drippings with crumbled bacon. Any kind of meat will provide the flavor and will be compatible with wine, although meats alone do nothing to help with the dryness of an otherwise bare salad.

Cheeses are another alternative, particularly if you use some more flavorful than those drab processed cheese hunks that you get in bulk at the supermarket. Nuts—almonds, walnuts, filberts—can add variety.

Of course, the ultimate solutions are to toss the tossed salad completely . . . or, as some people do, dash a little table vin into the romaine.

Chapter Twenty-one

Children and wine

ONE reason that many Americans only learn to appreciate wine during their late 20s or 30s is that we so seldom encountered it as children. During childhood, few of us drank wine as a table beverage, so we began to study the subject as adults after our fascination with beer and cocktails had run its course.

We studied because we had the time, the money, and the developing taste, and because we were often embarrassed by our ignorance of it in social situations.

Perhaps we could blame our parents for our inexperience. After all, even in a fairly dry household, I learned the pleasures of bourbon but not the pleasures of Burgundy. Still, our parents shouldn't be totally faulted. Few of us would have been taken by California wines available in post-Prohibition days, and who could afford fine French imports during the Depression?

If this lack of childhood training of our generation is explainable, will the next generation fare any better?

Among wine-loving friends who have families, I am surprised to find few of them regularly serve children wine at meals. And I suspect this abstinence is the rule. How else can we explain the popularity of "pop" wines a few years ago? It follows that only kids who were not familiar with good wines would drink such inferior fare.

One reason parents may be reluctant to serve children wine is the lingering Puritan notion that wine "will not be good for them," even though the healthful properties of wine have long been known. But even the ancients knew nothing of its value as a source of vitamins and as a killer of harmful bacteria. Wine is far short of being any wonder drug, but it is interesting to note that Canadian scientists have discovered that phenols present in wine pigment can kill viruses, including those that cause polio.

The list of potential dangers is short—alcohol. Obviously, no one wants growing children to be tipplers and, in fact, teenage alcoholism is a serious problem. But the root of juvenile drinking problems seems to be in surreptitious drinking, not in sensible consumption at family meals. As a student of mine once explained: "I'm Italian, and our family always had wine, so who wanted to go out and drink wine to rebel? There were other ways to get in trouble."

However, the amount to be consumed is a consideration. An average adult may be able to drink a bottle a day and suffer no long-term damage (as scientific studies indicate), but a child's portion must be limited according to age or size. The Europeans get around this quite nicely by cutting the wine with water, although it would be a shame to dilute a really fine wine.

It would be a shame also if your child's first exposures to wine were negative. For that reason, go easy on the strong or tannic wines such as Bordeaux, Rhônes, Burgundies, and Barolos. In time youngsters will probably be able to appreciate these fine reds, but start them out on wines that have some fruitiness and a hint of sweetness, such as Vouvray,

Beaujolais, and Moselle Spätlese. A not-too-dry sparkling wine will also appeal to young tastes.

While the kids are developing a taste for wines, they can also develop a knowledge of them. Some parents encourage their children to discuss the merits of particular wines as they are served and how well they match the foods. The table is also a logical place to discuss sensible drinking, much more so than a police station after your drunken offspring has totalled your new BMW.

If you want to be a really thoughtful parent and make up for all the things you missed as a child, consider the English practice of laying down a "birthday vintage" of wine. For example, if your child was born in 1970, lay away a case of a fine 1970 wine to be enjoyed by her when she and the wine reach maturity. It's a delightful practice, but one that is becoming more threatened as vintners make their wines to mature in less than a dozen years.

However, the better Médocs can still last for 20 years, and you should consider them for children born in 1966, 1970, and 1975. Vintage Port can easily improve for 25 years, and children who were born in 1966, 1967, 1975, and especially 1970, are fortunate if these are laid down for them.

What better way to cement the generation gap than to deliver a case of vintage Port or Médoc to your son or daughter on some special occasion such as a wedding or college graduation? And, if you have trained them well at the table, they will have the palates to truly appreciate your gifts.

PART FOUR
Having Fun with Wine

Chapter Twenty-two

You and the restaurant wine list

OFTEN people who have recently become interested in wines assume that, with a modest knowledge of regions and vintages, they can easily cope with restaurant wine lists.

This is only partly true. Eternal vigilance (and a little forethought) in the pursuit of a reasonably priced, reasonably drinkable restaurant wine may be more helpful than carefully memorized *grand crus* and closely watched vintages.

There are three obstacles that even a knowledgeable and vigilant wine drinker faces: overpricing, poor wine and poor wine service, and the law of differing dishes, which says that the number of people in your party ordering dishes that demand different wines is equal to the number of people in your party.

Overpricing is almost the rule in restaurants, although a few wise owners are bucking this ultimately self-defeating practice. The most obvious way to combat this robbery is to buy cheap, although even many veteran drinkers are embarrassed to order a serviceable, although undistinguished, table wine.

You have to ask yourself if a *cru* Bordeaux in an off year is worth $25 when you could buy it off the shelf for $6. Better to buy the nonvintage California Cabernet for $7. Expensive wines also have a slower turnover rate and will suffer, particularly the whites, by improper storage. They may also have passed their peaks. This is particularly true of restaurant wines bought on sale and which are approaching that great tasting room in the sky.

With French wines, it is often wise to buy a regional shipper's wine (B & G, Louis Latour, Faiveley) rather than an estate-bottled wine. Not only is the shipper's wine less expensive, it is often a better wine in a poor year, as the shipper can "elevate" the wine through blending, something the estate bottler cannot do.

If there are no inexpensive bottles on the menu, inquire about the house carafe wine. Although many places routinely stock insipid California jug wines, a few restaurants take pride in finding inexpensive but good bulk wine, particularly from Italy.

Asking about the house wine as a matter of routine is not a bad idea anyway, as it gives you the opportunity to find out if the waiter and captain have any wine knowledge. Don't assume they do, no matter how good the wine list. If the staff is knowledgeable, then you might be steered to a good wine.

Neither does a good wine list indicate good storage conditions, but there is little remedy to this except to send back a wine that has oxidized or separated. One way to protect yourself is to ask the vintage if it is not stated. Be wary of atrocious vintages (such as Bordeaux 1968), white wines that are too old, and tannic reds that are too young.

Order your wine early and insist that it be brought to your table early, certainly before any food arrives. This gives you time to cope with, or eliminate, a number of potential disasters: a bad wine that has to be sent back, a white that needs time to chill (or that needs rescue from being chilled to death), a red that needs time to breathe, or, sin of sins, wine that arrives after you've been served an entree, which is quickly getting cold.

There are three ways of coping with the needs of your party. The most tricky one, but one that can be fun, is searching for one or two wines that can be "stretched" to cover all the dishes ordered. A knowledgeable wine waiter is at his best in this situation. Don't be tempted to try to have one wine cover beef and delicate shellfish, but veal or chicken with a heavier sauce might be paired with a light beef dish. (What wine would you choose, if available?) A good rule when stretching a wine's limits is to pick the lightest common denominator. It is better to have a wine in the background of a heavy dish than have a heavy wine obliterate a light dish.

A second solution is to order half bottles. Don't hesitate to ask if they are available, as some restaurants don't uniformly put all of them on the lists. Or you might order an excess of white, if you have a simple white-red division, in place of cocktails or to go with appetizers. The extra can carry over to the main course, with red being ordered for everyone else.

If you find none of these suggestions workable in coping with the problems of getting good wine at a good price, consider a substitute which at times can be almost as difficult to find today in restaurants—a large, cold glass of water.

Chapter Twenty-three

Summer wines for summer times

MUSIC whispers over the grass at Wolf Trap. Picnic baskets fill the woods around the canal path. The suburban air is redolent of charcoal. Sails off the cape, blankets on the beach, and late-morning mists in mountain coves—summer is fully here.

The enjoyment of wine moves outdoors, too. Summer's picnics, barbecues, and garden parties demand that wines be livelier, more refreshing and lighter. This is not the milieu of Lafite and Côte Rôtie. It is a time for wines that can be drunk chilled or cooled, for wines that are simple and inexpensive.

Although summer wines may share some characteristics, including lightness, freshness, and reasonable prices, the variety can match most moods and menus. Consider these:

Rosés are alfresco wines, and there is little excuse for them at any other time or place, although the wine effeterie, who would rather be caught with a copy of *The National Enquirer* in their shopping carts than a bottle of demi-rouge, can be tedious in their denunciations.

Most of us are familiar with the pleasant but rather uniform Portuguese rosé duo, Mateus and Lancer's But warm weather calls us to adventure and new paths. One such route leads to France, where you can judge for yourself whether the slightly sweet and rounded Rosé d'Anjou is better than the crisper, orange-tinted rosé from Tavel. If you're lucky enough to find a bottle of a Marsanny rosé from Burgundy, then you can have a three-way tasting for the pink crown of France and perhaps the world.

Neither are the California rosés to be ignored. One of the best pink wines I have tasted is Souverain's Pinot Noir Rosé 1977, which has an enticing honeysuckle fragrance and which is very fresh, fruity, and rather dry. A different taste is Robert Mondavi's Gamay Rosé 1976 with its pungent nose, tingling taste, and appealing-though-odd bubble gum flavor.

Rosés made from California's Cabernet Sauvignon grapes too often have elements that fight each other, almost as if resisting the making of a common wine from this royal grape.

White meats and lighter red meats are for rosé, as long as there isn't a spicy or heavy barbecue sauce to overpower them.

When your appetite for rosé pales, consider the light whites. Since white wines are meant to be cooled or chilled, there is a temptation to include practically all of them on a picnic list, excepting the dessert wines. But, as with most classifications, one can arrive at a category of ideal whites to drink in hot weather. First, they should be light (eliminate the Burgundians of the Côte d'Or) without being austere (toss out the Chablis). A bit of fragrance or floweriness would make things perfect.

There are some California, Loire, and German wines which immediately come to mind. To begin at home, one could hardly wish for a better wine than Callaway's Chenin Blanc, although it is a bit expensive for frivolous drinking. But it is certainly worth the price—a lovely platinum gold robe, spicy nose, a quick piquancy on the tongue that mellows with just the right touch of oak—not even enough wood to scare off those oak-haters who have nightmares of David Bruce.

At the other end of the price spectrum is Sebastiani's Green Hungarian. For some reason even the Sebastiani publicists seem to ignore this serviceable, very pleasant everyday wine.

As a class, you might want to sample the California Johannisberg Rieslings, particularly from Napa and Sonoma.

Sticking with Rieslings, you could practically walk blindfolded into your store's German wine section and come out with an extremely good bottle. If you wish to be more selective, choose a 1976 over a 1975 (which is like choosing a Mercedes over a Jaguar), get a Kabinett grade (the Spätlese and Auslese, while delicious, are going to be too sweet except for dessert), and look for a green-bottled Moselle, which will be a little more flowery than the better Rhines. If you don't like flowers, buy a Steinberger Kabinett. If you love floweriness, then buy a Liebfraumilch (Blue Nun will do fine) or get a Müller-Thurgau and Sylvaner mix from Nahe. Try the Kreuznacher Kroenenberg.

On to the Loire. Most Loire drinkers are up-river or down-river partisans. I'm a down-river partisan, which means that I am especially fond of the crisp yet flavorful Muscadet, and one of the best of the bunch is Domaine de L'Hyvernière Muscadet de Sèvre-et-Maine.

The up-river people go for the somewhat fuller and sometimes sweeter Vouvray, and you can play the game of trying to guess the exact taste each new batch of this fickle wine will bring. If you're lucky, you may still be able to buy a case of Ackerman's Cuvée St.-Paul 1976 for less than $40.

No barbecue for these, but try deli-style sandwiches and chilled chicken or tuna salads.

Red wines, like children, are often sent away for the summer, but this should only be the case if the reds, like children, are heavy, ponderous and brooding.

If you need a red wine to go with your hamburgers and barbecue meats, and you will, then a chilled Beaujolais can be your all-around handyman. Look for recent—but not always most recent—vintages.

For everyday Beaujolais, try Beaujolais Jadot, although the prices are often not everyday. As long as you're going to spend considerable money, throw in another dollar or so and work your way through the nine *cru* villages of Beaujolais: Pleurie, Brouilly, Morgon, and so on.

You may decide to stop permanently at Moulin-à-Vent, particularly if you can find a few bottles of a good vintage bottled by Fianson, generally a remarkably flavorful wine. If you want to vary tastes, try the less fruity and more peppery Bardolino, a light, refreshing Italian wine bottled in the area west of Venice. As with most of its wines, Bolla sells a good product at a reasonable price.

Most flavored wines have the original sin of not quenching one's thirst. That aside, there are some interesting wines that you might want to have on hand should the urge to drink a diet cola suddenly strike you.

Try instead a German May Wine, a light white that has a pleasant touch of the herb woodruff. Pour some in one of those oversized wine glasses and drop in a strawberry or two. Enjoy it, and quit being so fussy.

A slightly sweeter, fruitier concoction is the ubiquitous Sangria. Personally, whenever I taste Sangria, I get a horrible *déja vu* of pre-Christmas parties.

But, as they say, Sangria is a "fun wine," and everybody drinks it, even those of us who will take only a few sips before clearing our palates with nonvintage Jack Daniels.

Yago makes a tolerable import brand, but, as with sourdough bread, everyone has a favorite recipe for a syrup and/or liqueur base. To this base is added any leftover red jug wine that has not started to turn brown, plus some cut-up fruit.

Okay, if you must have it, don't make the base too sweet

(let the fruit take care of that), add a lot of peaches (to mellow the citrus peels), and spike it with some Triple Sec.

Sparkling Wines. And what could be more festive and romantic than a crackling cold bottle of sparkling wine enjoyed on the edge of a Degas meadow beside a Renoir stream? It will cost a bit more, but not necessarily a lot more, because sparkling wines come in many varieties and qualities.

One of the best buys is a French *vin mousseux* under the brand name "Kriter." It goes for about $8, has the proper acidity that most brut lovers look for, but does lack a bit in flavor.

Slightly higher are the German sparkling wines which are called "Sekt," of which there are several brands. The Henkell Sekt Trocken (dry) is an enjoyable wine that sometimes commands close to Champagne prices.

And with Champagne, you can let yourself get out of hand by spending the kind of money that rightly should go toward buying great reds. Try the Bollinger Special Cuvée Brut or the Moët & Chandon "White Star" Extra Dry, both nonvintage. The Bollinger is fuller and fruitier, and the "White Star" has an almost "sooty" aftertaste as a result of its dryness. It is not a bad taste, but it could be unpleasant to some.

Those who must have a bit more sweetness would go for the almost cloying Asti Spumante, a clear case of muscat love. (It will go with melon.) In California, Chandon and Schramsberg are the class sparkling wines. The foxier New York State varieties that masquerade on all of those "champagne" flights to Florida are less expensive as a class, but they show it.

If there are wines that go with almost everything, then it is the Champagne-styled wines. A bottle to whet the appetite served with a can of pâté from Strasbourg is a great way to start an outdoors extravaganza—and a second bottle with strawberries and cream is a good way of ending it.

Chapter Twenty-four

Serving wines during the holidays

MOST of the year we treat our wine reverently and lovingly, cradling it to make certain no sediment stirs, protecting it from the harmful vibrations of the washer and dryer, monitoring its table temperature like a fragile child filled with fever.

Then, during the winter holidays, we go a bit mad and roast wine, set wine on fire, and mix it with other spirits as though it were a common gin or vodka. We even put giant ice sculptures in huge bowls of it.

But the lunacy will do us good, and, if we are a bit fearful of this sacrilege, we can take solace in the fact that such acts of wine paganism during the holy days are traditional.

When in 1920 the late English wine lover and scholar George Saintsbury had published his *Notes on a Cellar-Book*, he described one such holiday tradition—a drink called "bishop."

"It is, as I have found more people not know than know in this ghastly thin-faced time of ours, simply mulled Port," he groused. "You take a bottle of that noble liquor and put it in a saucepan, adding as much or as little water as you can

99

reconcile to your taste and your conscience, an orange cut in half (I believe some people squeeze it slightly), and plenty of cloves (you may stick them in the orange if you have a mind).

"Sugar or no sugar at your discretion, and with regard to the character of the wine. Put it on the fire, and as soon as it is warm, and begins to steam, light it. The flames will be of an imposing infernal colour, quite different from the light blue flicker of spirits or of claret mulled. Before it has burned too long pour it in a bowl, and drink it as hot as you like. It is an excellent liquor, and I have found it quite popular with the ladies."

Saintsbury, who would never think of punning about a Port in every girl, goes on to describe the ecclesiastical family of mulled wines, a "cardinal" being "a rather silly name for mulled Claret," while a "pope" comes out a mulled Burgundy, which shows how the English rated their French wines at the beginning of the century.

"*No* Burgundy," he noted, "is really suitable for mulling, while to mull a good Burgundy is a capital crime."

To remain with Saintsbury for a moment: "It (mulling Burgundy) is quite different from *vin brûlé*, a popular beverage in old France, and a regular Christmas and New Year's tradition in the Channel Islands. When made of an unpretentious Bordeaux, it wants no dilution, of course, and if it is a fairly stout wine, should want no fortifying. Some sugar it will certainly want, not to correct acidity, but to fill out body and flavour; a cloved and cloven lemon instead of the orange of the bishop, a saucepan, a fire, and goblets."

And we still make it that way today.

There are other varieties of heated wine drinks, a popular one being the Swedish *Glögg*, a concoction of red wine, sweet vermouth, and aquavit (about a half cup of each of the latter to a bottle of the former) spiced by cinnamon, cloves, sugar, orange slices, and topped off with raisins and almonds.

I once ran across a similar drink, *Glühwein*, while covering a ski festival some years ago. It was the first time I had tried a hot, spiced wine, and as I drank it in front of a warming fire I resolved to get the recipe. Somehow that night I never got around to it.

The French have a drink called grog, after an English admiral who wore a grogram coat and who ordered his men to cut their ration of rum by watering it. The French being French substituted wine for rum and heated it, making grog a more Gallic holiday drink than the Anglo mixture.

A truly English—well Gaelic—hot wine drink is wassail, from the phrase *was hael* or "be well," a toast that has largely passed from the language as we *skoal* all over the place. Anyway, wassail adds a cup of dry sherry and two cups of orange juice to the red wine, traditionally a claret (red Bordeaux), sometimes pineapple juice, plus cut lemons, sugar, and cinnamon. A syrup made of sugar, lemons, cinnamon, and some water is added to the above, and all are heated

Turning to cooler stuff, we have punches, which I must admit are generally not my cup of wine, as they are either over-sweet or puckeringly astringent. A rather elegant exception is *kalte Ente* which is German for "cold duck" (this is beginning to sound like a Bud and Travis routine), which has nothing to do with the insipid sparkling wine of the same name. *Kalte Ente* is made by stirring a few teaspoons of sugar and lemon juice together in a punch bowl and adding two bottles of Kabinett grade Moselle to one bottle of brut Champagne. The duck? Simply an ornament shaped from a peeled lemon.

Other punches are from such combinations as brandy, Cointreau, and sparkling water (one-half cup each) added to a bottle of Champagne; a California rosé of Zinfandel accompanied by apricots and a splash of Calvados; white Bordeaux with Grenadine syrup and a few dashes of orange liqueur.

The word "punch," incidentally, is said to derive from a Hindustani term, *paunch*, picked up by English sailors. Paunch means five and stood for the original five elements of the concoction—spirits, water, sliced citrus, sugar, and spice. With the exception of minor substitutions, we really haven't strayed that much from the basic concept.

Similar to punches are the English cups, wherein fruit, herbs, or liqueurs are added to iced wine. However, these are generally considered summer coolers more than winter warmers.

Should all these popes and bishops, Glöggs and Glühweins, punches and wassails seem too much trouble, then test the range of sparkling wines to float you from pre-Christmas soirées to New Year's Eve parties.

Who knows, they might provide you with enough imagination to invent your own traditional Christmas wine drink.

Chapter Twenty-five

Parlor games

BACK in our early teens, when we hoped that the changes in our voices would match the changes in our physiology, the hot game at Friday night parties was spin the bottle. Generally it was a Coke bottle, but, if we were feeling daring, it might be a Blue Ribbon long necker.

The object of the game was to have the teetering bottle stop so that it was pointing at the giggling girl with blue eyes and blonde hair, although we might lose the nerve to kiss her if it did.

If there is still some adolescence in you, there is another type of parlor game you can play with a bottle. It may not provide the thrill that kissing young blue eyes would, but the bottle does have its sweet mysteries, too.

Blind tasting—trying to evaluate and guess the contents of a disguised bottle—is not related to blind man's buff, although the tactics may be similar. And it's surrounded by tales of legendary prowess which would put the backseat braggadocio of your youth to shame.

Have you heard the one about the guy who instantly

recognized the 1964 Château Palm Air on the first sip, as well as identifying the angle of the vineyard slope and the type of fungicides applied? He did miss the number of days the wine spent on the oak, however.

In most cases, a blind tasting is not totally blind. The taster may know that he is drinking eight 1973 Bordeaux and the names of each estate. Or it may be seven different vintages of Château Gloria. In either case, the task is to sort out which glass is which. The way to do this is by deduction, taking what you know and applying it against what you taste.

It isn't easy. At one tasting for a wine society not long ago, we were given six California reds and six California whites, each of a different variety of grape. To make the task easier, we tasted three at a time, knowing which three, but not in what order. Even so, less than a tenth of the tasters could sort out all 12 wines. The biggest stumbling block was the Chardonnay, normally an easy variety to recognize, but whose traits were masked because the wine was too cold.

The techniques of blind tastings are easy. The labels are masked, but it is preferable in cross-varietal or cross-regional tastings that not even the bottle be shown, as the shape or color can tip off the taster. The glasses may be numbered as well.

Why blind taste at all? It's necessary in wine-judging competition where even the most objective judge might be swayed if he knew what he was drinking. Generally, though, blind tastings are just for the fun of it, with perhaps some learning value thrown in. Games keep us occupied and off the streets, and the deductive process can make us apply what we think we know.

Except for experts and rabid drinkers, blind tastings generally are too stuffy and formal, so here are some variations on the theme which can provide an interesting evening of drinking and game playing. The degree of difficulty should relate to the degree of knowledge of your guests.

Try your mouth at these:

Name That Varietal. Choose four California whites and four California reds—say, Chardonnay, Riesling, Chenin Blanc, Sauvignon Blanc, Cabernet Sauvignon, Pinot Noir, Merlot, and Zinfandel. If your guests are knowledgeable, tell them no more and present the four whites for identification and the four reds. If they are relative novices, read what each varietal should taste like from a wine primer.

The person who guesses the most right should be given a prize. The best prizes are not books, but a bottle of wine, which, one would hope, will be shared on the spot.

Twenty Questions. Have each guest bring a bottle, perhaps specifying red or white so you will have an equal number in deference to those who don't want to drink all of either for the evening. Have the bottles concealed in paper bags.

Each person will have to guess one wine, obviously not the one he brought, although everyone will be poured a glass. The player then has to guess the wine by asking questions which can be answered "yes" or "no." When he has chosen correctly (the actual vintage would be asking too much), then go on to the next bottle player. The person who needs the fewest questions to identify his bottle wins.

If you're intent or. giving a book, try *Pride of the Wineries,* a regional analysis of California wines.

The Price Is Right. Choose six white wines (or reds) of varying costs from jug wines to higher priced bottles. Similar styles would be preferable, but not necessary. The person who gets the right price order—most expensive to least expensive—wins. The prize? A jug of Gallo Gewürztraminer.

The Newly Rich Game. Ask your guests to identify which wine is from a classic region of France and which is a comparable upstart from California. The pairings might be a Médoc and a Cabernet Sauvignon, a red Burgundy and a Pinot Noir, a white Burgundy and a Chardonnay, and a white Graves and a Sauvignon Blanc. For a prize, a bottle of 1977 Hacienda Cabernet.

Blind tastings, whether played for fun, as the ones suggested above, or played seriously, also serve to teach beginners, who learn as the expert in the room explains his deductions as he goes along or after the fact.

The only problem is that someone has to mask the bottles and keep track of what is being poured. Numbering paper bags after the bottle has been inserted and shuffled around is one answer. Having a butler or a maid is another.

Or you may want to enlist your teenage son or daughter who has the time and temperament to keep the old folks amused by playing games with them.

That is, if they're not out playing spin the bottle.

Chapter Twenty-six

How to hold a wine tasting

WINE tasting.

Do those two words conjure up an image of effete bores, nose over glass, eyebrow touching eyebrow, scribbling indecipherable notes, and mumbling, "Something must have gone wrong in the latter stages of malolactic fermentation"?

Or, worse, of those horrid commercial affairs where some guy in two-tone shoes drinks with one hand while smoking with the other, telling the world that he likes Blue Nun with everything?

Fortunately, there is a way to have a wine tasting party where you can drink good wine and talk good talk without snobbery or great expense.

Begin by inviting three or four couples who like wine but are not fanatics (they spoil everyone's fun). Next, forget about food until the day of the party and then buy three or four kinds of mild cheese (nothing runny or blue-veined), Norwegian flatbread or a loaf of French bread, and something simple for dessert.

Don't ask guests to bring wine. They might fetch something horrid or you might wind up with seven bottles of the same wine. It's your party.

To narrow possibilities, try four white wines followed by four reds. Pick light or dry ones in each category and some full ones. Plan to serve them in order from lightest white to fullest white, then light red to full red. If a wine surprises you by being fuller than the one that follows, it will not cause a scandal.

You might begin with something simple such as eight French or eight Californians or a world sampler. Don't be tempted by vertical or horizontal tastings. In a vertical, the same or similar wines are presented in a number of vintages—'63, '69, '72, and so on. A horizontal is of several similar wines (eight Médocs, for example) of the same year. The problem with these tastings is that there is little variety for guests, who might not get the nuances of the limited tastings anyway. The point is to enjoy.

A simple but varied tasting might run thus: Muscadet, Graves Blanc, Hermitage Blanc, Meursault, Chinon, Morgon, Margaux, Hermitage. Each guest will probably find a wine or two worthy of buying later. Californians? Try Johannisberg Riesling, Chenin Blanc, Sauvignon Blanc (also Fumé Blanc), Chardonnay, Gamay Beaujolais, Petite Sirah, Zinfandel, Cabernet Sauvignon.

Procedurally, set up two stemmed glasses for each guest in the serving area. Have a stack of napkins handy for wiping the last few drops from a glass before proceeding to the next. (Rinsing glasses is too fussy.) A large plastic bowl can hold used napkins and any leftover wine.

Fix yourself a brief schedule so that each red will be open about thirty minutes before being poured. And, don't forget to pop the whites in the fridge two hours before guests arrive.

The host should pour each wine, certainly no more than a quarter-glass. Normally, a bottle can serve eight to ten people with some left over.

Take about fifteen or twenty minutes with each wine. Expect some comments with each new bottle, but the conversation will probably ramble off on some other topic. Don't overwhelm with wine talk.

I always provide sheets with the wines typed on and a stack of pencils. Some people will jot down comments on all wines. More likely, a guest will merely check a certain wine on the list for later use. I make my notes in the kitchen before pouring. This way a bad or inferior bottle can be replaced before serving.

When the whites are gone, bring out fresh glasses for the reds and continue. Once you've run the gamut of wines, invite the guests to resample for a few minutes. Conversation about wines may also lead you to run down to the cellar for a particular bottle.

Finally, it's dessert time, and perhaps a change of venue to the table or to another room. Have plenty of hot, fresh coffee. Then trot your guests off . . . happy, but sober.

Chapter Twenty-seven

Tapa parties

To the student of primitive culture, the word "tapa" refers to a type of cloth made from bark by natives of Pacific Islands.

The wine lover has a different image, for "tapa" also refers to the ever-present canapés in the bars and cafes of Madrid and Jerez that accompany the mandatory afternoon glass of very dry sherry.

But tapas are more than a type of food to the Spaniards. They are part of the social custom where families, friends, and neighbors congregate after the working day is over to talk politics or sports or simply watch the parade of strollers. Many tourists, including this one, have found the hours of the tapa one of the most memorable aspects of the country.

It is a custom that is easily transferable to America. A tapa party is an easy substitute for a cocktail party, and a welcome one as more and more social drinkers switch from liquor to wine. Whether held as a weekend afternoon buffet or a nighttime event, a tapa party is an excellent occasion to feature Spanish wines as well as Spanish food.

For tapas, the Spanish particularly like thin slices of sun-cured ham, prawns and other seafood, olives, and grilled onions. Some other tapas you might try are almonds, cheeses, mushrooms, sausages, and shrimp. For convenience, prepare everything in bite-sized portions and forego anything more complex than finger food. A light grilling under the broiler can be the finishing touch to many of the foods.

A bar consisting of a half-dozen or more Spanish wines will allow guests to sample at their leisure. Sherry, the primary wine, is traditionally sipped from a *copita*, a small stemmed glass that narrows sharply toward the top to hold in the aroma, although any wine glass will do.

Spanish wines are generally inexpensive and increasingly available, but you may find the breadth of wines at your store to be somewhat narrow. With a little shopping around, however, you should be able to find representatives of most regions or types.

Sherry represents a small portion of Spanish wine production but it is the most familiar to Americans. It comes from the area of Jerez on the Atlantic Ocean, and much of it is aged and blended in England. Essentially, it is a fortified wine with alcohol added to raise it to around 17–20 percent, considerably higher than the normal 10–13 percent for unfortified wines. Sherry can be very sweet or very dry. You'll want the latter—known as *fino*—to serve with tapas. Perhaps the best is Gonzales Byass' Tio Pepe and Pedro Domecq's La Ina. Sherry-like wines from nearby Manzanilla and Montilla are also available.

Moving to the north of Spain, we come to the wines of Rioja, which are often likened to the Bordeaux but are perhaps more closely akin to Rhône wines. The reds are the best, ranging from the light but flavorful claretes to the darker tintos to the well-aged (and more expensive) reservas. Among the better Riojas are Marqués de Romeral and Marqués de Riscal, but I also enjoy the Paternina and Cuné lines.

White Riojas are less distinctive, although, at their best, they have the dry tanginess of a fresh Soave.

Similar to Rioja, but never reaching the heights of the best reservas, is the Torres brand of red wines from Catalonia on the Mediterranean in the Barcelona area. The cheapest of these is the famous Sangre de Toro or bull's blood, a good everyday wine. Torres also makes higher-priced reds under the names Coronas and Gran Coronas.

Remaining in Catalonia, we come to Spain's best sparkling wines, particularly those of the village of San Sadurni de Noya. While not as good as Champagne, they are pleasant, affordable wines with a character all their own. For example, I recently purchased a Freixenet Cordon Negro for the unbelievable price of $2.99. It was full and fragrant with a woody taste and nose. Its fragrance, both in nose and taste, was that of (honest to God) a geranium leaf or a desert shrub such as an ocotillo. (At least I'm not claiming violets and truffles.) It is well worth trying.

It seems that every European capital has its favorite everyday wine—Muscadet for Paris, Frascati for Rome, Gumpoldskirchner for Vienna. In Madrid, the cafe wine is Valdepeñas, a light but alcoholic red (although some white is made) that appears on your table, often without being ordered, with lunch or dinner in much the same way that American restaurants used to provide a mandatory glass of water. Valdepeñas is light, fruity, guzzable and comes from La Mancha, the plain south of Madrid. Hopefully, no one at your party will be moved to sing "The Impossible Dream" or to fight any unbeatable foes.

Last and least is Sangria, one of my least favorite wines, Spanish or otherwise. The wine-and-citrus drink can be served as an iced alternative for those who miss their tea on the rocks.

Chapter Twenty-eight

Wines for tailgate parties

YOU might munch an overpriced hot dog at a baseball game or chew on a salty pretzel at a basketball game, but it is football—particularly college football—that allows you to have a comfortable luncheon, watch a contest, and then leisurely have dessert and drinks.

I speak of course of the tailgater, that fall institution that originated back when we had caravans of gas-guzzling station wagons that now may follow the rumble seat and running board into extinction. But the tailgater is here to stay, particularly on college campuses where huge green parking lots allow us to spread out an extravaganza of food. And wine.

The interesting thing about the college football season is that you begin with baked September heat and end with cold December winds. What we eat and drink at the first tailgater, when our hopes are high, varies considerably from game eleven, when our bodies, and sometimes hopes, are quite chilled.

Warm weather tailgating is very much like a summertime

113

picnic. Cold cuts, fresh vegetables, and fried chicken are the order of the day, and so are chilled, light, fruity wines.

At minimum, you should bring along at least one white and one red rosé on ice. For the white, why not break out a sparkling wine from California to toast the new season? Or a sparkling Vouvray—or even a still one? This is also the time for fruity, inexpensive German wines. The charm of a superior grade 1976 Moselle or Rhine would be lost, but a recent, simple Qualitätswein from the same region could give a flowery touch to your picnic. There are also some reasonably priced whites from Württemberg appearing on the dealers' shelves as well. From California, you might want a medium-priced Chenin Blanc. Another good Californian is J. Lohr's proprietary brand "Jade," a mixture of Johannisberg Riesling, Gewürztraminer, and Sylvaner.

As far as reds are concerned, chilled Beaujolais is ideal early fall fare. Bardolino or Valpolicella are good alternatives. The California wineries are also experimenting a lot these days with rosés and with whites made from red grapes. In both cases, those vinted from the Zinfandel grape show a lot of taste and promise. Again, a picnic is the perfect occasion to try these more casual wines.

As the weather gets colder, the food—and wines—become more substantial. Many people who tailgate drive elaborate vans with kitchens to allow the cooking of food on the premises, a bit ostentatious perhaps, but welcome on a cool autumn afternoon.

Sturdy whites, such as everyday Chardonnays, become the wines of the weekend, as do more substantial, if not elegant, reds. The subtleties of fine California Cabernets and Zinfandels, or fine wines from Bordeaux and Burgundy, would be lost in the revelry, but a hearty Petite Sirah from California will warm the heart and stomach. Other possibilities are lesser Riojas, the minor Rhône wines, and the northern Italian reds, excepting better Chiantis, Barolos, and Amarones.

Many of us like to linger after the game to replay the action and avoid the traffic. Perfect time for brandy, but why not a Port for dessert and warmth? If you don't want to pay the price of a true vintage Port, then take the opportunity to try the very respectable and reasonably priced nonvintage, California, Port-style wine from Ficklin.

A decent but not extravagant dessert white wine from the Moselle or from Sauternes (or a Barsac) are good alternatives.

If budgeting is a consideration in your tailgating, another way to approach your selection is to try some of the inexpensive (for now) wines from areas not yet popular with the world's drinkers. Italian wines, for example, have already begun to creep up in price and are not the comparative bargain they were just a couple of years ago.

South American wines from Chile and Argentina particularly have begun to flood the market and are still good bargains. In some cases the Cabernets and Rieslings are especially good.

There are also some minor Portuguese reds and whites becoming available for the first time. Many of the reds are particularly interesting because they have several years of wood and bottle age—not elegant, but not jug wines either.

In short, tailgaters call for the more casual wines that the atmosphere dictates and provide an opportunity to try some of the lesser-known bottles. Which will also help accentuate the thrill of victory and deaden the agony of defeat.

Chapter Twenty-nine

Wine and travel

FROM time to time we see articles in which wine authorities are asked to name their most memorable bottle of wine, the presumption being the respondent will name a rare and classic growth sipped in solitude in the confines of his private cellar. Occasionally it is, but more often the expert will fondly tell of a fairly common bottle of wine enjoyed in the romantic atmosphere of some exotic place.

In my case, one of the most memorable bottles—but by no means the best—was a very good Fleurie, a Beaujolais, drunk with a picnic lunch of French country pâté in a quiet corner of the gardens at Versailles one day in late spring when the birds were singing and other tourists were nowhere to be seen.

Wine and travel: an ideal combination, but one often overlooked by vacationers, particularly those who feel constrained by the limits of a structured group tour. But even that rigid structure need not spoil your pursuit of good wine.

A first rule should be to try wines—common or rare—that you do not ordinarily find in your local wine store. A Valdepeñas in Madrid is an example of the former; a Château Grillet in the Rhône Valley is an example of the latter.

Another rule is that it's seldom worth the bother to buy wine abroad to bring back to the United States yourself—unless money and bulky suitcases are no problem. Wine bought abroad is generally no bargain, particularly in France where taxes are high and exchange rates unfavorable. If you find something there you really like, it can be an interesting challenge to look for it back home. Your wine merchant will help; so will Harry Rubin who writes the "Wine Press" column for *Gourmet*.

One of the best ways to enjoy wine abroad is the aforementioned picnic. My wife and I have had many delightful lunches featuring wine this way: in the Retiro in Madrid after a morning of Rubens and Valasquez at the nearby Prado; in Chapultepec Park in Mexico City on an Easter weekend; in the Bois de Boulogne near the outskirts of Paris. It takes a bit of planning ahead, but that can be fitted into your itinerary. An evening walk before dinner can include a stop at a wine store near your hotel, and a neighborhood grocery, not a rarity in most European downtown sections, can provide canned or nonperishable food for the next day's lunch.

Should picnics not be your style, carefully study the wine menu at lunch and dinner, looking for local wines. They are often the least expensive. There are interesting, if not outstanding, local wines in such unlikely cities as Toronto and Acapulco. In the latter instance, the high Mexican taxes on imported wines will make the domestic ones taste even better. The cities of Spain, Italy, France, Portugal, Germany, and most Eastern European countries provide classic possibilities. Check your wine book before you leave or ask the maître d' at the restaurant.

Then there is total involvement. If you have an extra day in Paris, try a local bus tour to the châteaux of the Loire Valley or the caves of Champagne. You can hardly miss the brochures in your hotel lobby, but your concierge can help if you need it. Similar tours exist in Spain and other major wine countries.

Even more involved are total package tours of wine regions. Some of the more expensive might include the wine and food of France or Italy and last for several days. Some feature famous wine writers and other knowledgeable people to explain what you are drinking and how it got that way. One trip—an intriguing one that I have not tried—features a barge tour of the canals of north-central France and advertises dock-side visits to local restaurants and wineries as you slowly float through rustic countryside. Your travel agent will be more than glad to provide details.

Individualists who prefer to rent a car drive the backroads of Burgundy and the wine roads of Germany at their leisure. In this instance I recommend studying one of the special guides for this purpose before you leave home. Two especially good ones dealing with France are by Frederick S. Wildman, Jr., *Wine Tour of France*, and Frederick Tingey, *Wine Roads of France*. Both have maps and give precise instructions on where you can drink, eat, and sleep (hotels, inns, campgrounds). The Wildman book is the more interesting, as it deals with the history of each area and of the wines made there.

Domestic wine tourists should not forget the Napa Valley just a couple of hours north of San Francisco by car. Most of the wineries give lectures and tastings. Off-season (before June, after August) is best here, as the weekend traffic jams in downtown Rutherford can be horrendous.

Whatever your method, marrying wine with your travel can be informative and romantic. Perhaps it is because of the latter consideration that wine writers often say that this wine or that wine does not travel well—that is, it tastes better at its origin than at its destination. The fact that a cool bottle of Frascati may be more appealing in an outdoor cafe in Rome than in your dining room in Nashville may have nothing to do with the rigors of transit.

Chapter Thirty

The romance of wine

WE had been following the yellow-and-blue balloon for almost an hour as it floated low over the Amish farmlands north of Lancaster, Pennsylvania. The figure in red occasionally waved from its aerie in the wicker gondola under the towering, hot-air envelope.

After a while, the acetylene burner heaved its last dragon's-breath sigh, and the pilot and passenger in red glided slowly down toward a green meadow. We rushed from the tracking car toward the balloon as it bumped down and tottered, the bag slowly losing its air. Hands quickly wrestled the deflated balloon, now straightening, now folding, until it was packed snugly into the empty gondola.

At last it was time for the post-flight Champagne—actually Domaine Chandon Napa Valley Blanc de Noirs—and the passenger in red, exuberant at her maiden balloon flight, drank the first toast . . .

Very often, we take wine too seriously, getting wrapped up with issues like acid balance, proper cellar temperature and must weight. But we should remember that wine is the drink of romance and romantics. Here are a few scenarios to get you in the mood.

There's a small hotel. You don't have to go far to get away to a small country inn, wherever you live. A couple of years ago, we spent a weekend at the 1740 House along the Delaware River in Bucks County, Pennsylvania, where there are several inns. The 1740, like some other small hotels, has no liquor license, so we took along a Chardonnay and a red Bordeaux to match whatever entree was being served in their small dining room. A *fino* sherry also went along for sipping in our room. After a quiet, delicious meal (we chose the Chardonnay), there was a moonlight stroll up the country road to the Black Bass Hotel with its pewter bar from Paris.

In the wilderness. Take the time to search for a perfect spot in the boondocks along a small stream, pick a perfect day when puffy white clouds dot the sky, and pack a picnic lunch— cheeses, fruit, pâté. Bring along a crystal vase (or even a Mateus bottle) for some freshly picked daisies. Oh yes, the wine. Ice down some California *blancs de noirs* and rosés, wines that have just a touch of color and a little tannin for body. Sebastiani Eye of the Swan and Simi Rosé of Cabernet Sauvignon are good choices.

In concert. What goes better with wine and romance than music? You can make your own, or you can take in an outdoor concert at Tanglewood or Wolf Trap or some other place where wine drinking is permitted. Beaujolais is a good bet on a warm summer's night, and if you've never gotten around to trying the various *crus villages*, then what else for the occasion but a Beaujolais from Saint-Amour? In a more formal mood? Then it has to be the Boston Pops with its Champagne intermissions.

When in Rome (or Paris). One of the highlights of a recent trip to California had nothing to do with vineyards. Rather it was a mild October afternoon at Nepenthe's, a restaurant with an outdoor terrace that yielded a mountainside view of the Pacific Ocean below with waves pounding a Big Sur beach. A Monterey Peninsula wine was on our table. One of the joys of foreign travel, I think, is sampling the local wines in one of the famous old parks or gardens—the Retiro in Madrid with a Rioja, Hyde Park in London with a light white from Isle of Wight, the Versailles Gardens with a Bordeaux Blanc and a Fleurie are some personal examples.

Candlelight dinner for two. The classic. Scrape together whatever china, silver, and crystal you have, and if you don't have any, simply cut back on the number of candles and who can tell the difference. Veal rosemary and a Stags Leap Wine Cellars Haynes Vineyard Chardonnay can set the pace for a romantic Saturday night live, or, if your appetites are in a more Rabelaisian mood, a rare steak with a Carneros Creek Zinfandel.

Tramping in the vineyards. Looking toward fall, contact one of the local vineyards, whether you live in Virginia, Massachusetts, or Arkansas, and volunteer to pick grapes. Since only a fool turns down free labor, the two of you can spend a hazy Saturday afternoon snipping ripe bunches of grapes while killing your thirst with *vin ordinaire*. Note the varieties you're picking, and have the winemaker call you when the wine from these grapes is bottled. You'll have to pay, of course, but in a few months—or perhaps a year—the wine will be ready. Your love may have vanished by then, but you can drink to the sweet memories.

A little night music, I. You've had a satisfying evening at the theater, or you've just gotten home from a dinner party. You want to relax and discuss the evening. Kick off your shoes, loosen your tie (or whatever), and pour a small glass of vintage Port to sip. As supplies vary from store to store, ask your wine merchant to suggest one from the 1960, '63, or '66 vintages.

A little night music, II. Autumn is here, and the first frost is outside—time to break in the fireplace for another season. As the oak logs crackle and sing, bring out a crumbly cheese, turn out the lights, break out the bottle of fine burgundy you've been saving, and stretch out for the evening. Of course, it would be a waste not to finish the bottle.

A little night music, III. You're in a particularly romantic, wicked, or silly mood (whatever fits). Put on your Willie Nelson *Stardust* album, or Ravel, or Nick Lowe. A fresh bowl of strawberries dusted with powdered sugar on her side of the bed, and an ice bucket on yours. Chilling in the ice bucket: A light but sweet Saar, say a 1976 Ockfener Bockstein Spätlese. Who needs Johnny Carson?

All of this is rather contrived and silly, you say? Then take your glass of Mountain Chablis and hurry back to the television before the Superstars competition goes off.

Chapter Thirty-one

Your birth year— a vintage year?

THE summary record of vintages at Château Lafite-Rothschild for 1943 relates that the harvest began on September 19, that the quantity was *moyenne* (or average), and that the result was *bons vins quelques très grand réussites* (good wines some of which were very successful). Throughout Bordeaux, 1943 was recorded as a great year for both red and white wines.

Why the interest in 1943?

I'm 37 years old (as of this writing), and 1943 is the year of my birth. Like any adult who has ever passed idle conversation in a bar, I know my astrological sign (Gemini) and the animal sign of my birth year in the Chinese scheme of things (ram). So why not take the trouble to look up the vintage quality of my favorite year in my favorite wine region?

Much of our enjoyment of wine is whimsical and romantic. Practically any wine lover will freely admit that some of the best bottles he has tasted were with a beautiful woman in an enchanting setting. We buy wine, more than we would like to admit, on the basis of a label—either its looks or its prestige. We celebrate with festive sparkling wines, even when we would prefer something a little less fizzy.

So if I'm whimsical enough to take a tour of classic years, then perhaps you'll be whimsical enough to see if your birth year (or those of your spouse or children) is among them—if you haven't already looked it up.

Staying for a moment with French regions, where vintages are strictly observed, and with recent Port vintages, we can single out a few years in this century which by general consensus were simply amazing.

For example, if you were born in 1929 you might think negatively of your year because of some pretty crashing events on Wall Street. But it was a great year in Bordeaux—and Burgundy—and even along the Rhône and in Alsace, a combination of successes that rarely occurs in the meteorologically independent regions of France.

Or take 1945. Stellar in Bordeaux, along the Rhône, and in Alsace, as well as a vintage year in the Port lodges. How about 1947? Take a bow for the Bordeaux, white Burgundies, Champagnes, and Rhônes of '47. And 1955 was one of the best years across the board ever in France, as well as being one of the best vintage years for Port.

If you have a daughter born in 1966 or a son in '69, give them some respect. Both very good years.

But don't forget there were some horrendous years, when *tout le monde* was producing either horrendous or, at best, average stuff. I give you 1930, '31, '32, 1939, and 1941. Look for your glory elsewhere.

Scanning great vintages according to regions:

Bordeaux (red)—1920, '24, '28, '29, '34, '43, '45, '47, '49, '53, '55, '61, '62, '64, '66, '70, and '75.

Bordeaux (white)—'21, '28, '29, '37, '43, '45, '47, '49, '55, '61, '62, and '67.

Burgundy (red)—'15, '23, '28, '29, '37, '42, '47, '49, '55, '61, '64, '66, '69, and some would say '76.

Burgundy (white)—'29, '55, '69, and '70.

Champagne—'11, '21, '28, '47, '53, '64, and '66.

Rhône—'04, '29, '33, '45, '47, '49, '52, '54, '55, '57, '61, '67, and '69.

Alsace—'29, '34, '45, '49, '59, '61, '66, '67, '70, '71, and '73.

Recent declared vintages of Port by most shippers include '45, '55, '63, '66, and '70. Italian vintages of major wines have not been historically monitored that closely, but very good recent years include '64, '68, and '69 for Barolo, and '68, '71, and '75 for Chianti Classico.

California's serious winemaking has been so interrupted by politics (Prohibition), American tastes (sweet wines), and fragmentation (little estate bottling), that it is difficult to generalize on many vintages. But your kid born in 1973 or 1974 didn't pick a bad year.

Nor did your children born in 1976 or 1971 if you prefer the great nectary wines of the Mosel and the Rhine.

(The ancients also set a great deal of store in the "wines of the comet," or wines that were made in a year of great comet activity. Such a year, history tells us, was 1811. Unfortunately, the last year that Halley's Comet passed through— 1910—was not a great one anywhere in France. So much for the comet theory.)

But now that you have this whimsical information, what are you to make of it? Well, the parent of a child born in 1975 who lays down a case of good red Bordeaux for drinking on the heir's twenty-first birthday in 1996 will not be forgotten in old age.

If you're a bit more selfish—and I am—then you might look for wines of your birth year to drink as a curiosity piece on your birthday or other occasion. If you're an adult, you can forget about most white wines, and even some reds will have passed their prime. You might be able to find some Bordeaux, Burgundies, Rhônes (Hermitage, Côte Rôtie), and vintage Ports that are still enjoyable to drink—if you can afford to buy them once you've found them.

Personally, I've never sampled a 1943 wine from the Bordeaux or anywhere else, but I guess that's just one more pleasure to look forward to. One reason that I am encouraged is the Lafite registry. In 1943, Lafite harvested 112 *tonneaux* of grapes, which roughly translates into more than 10,000 cases or more than 120,000 bottles.

And I'll keep an eye out for the rest of the Médoc as well.

PART FIVE
How to
Be Master
(or Mistress)
of Your Cellar

Chapter Thirty-two

Starting a cellar

HAVE you ever thought about having a wine cellar, but didn't know where to start?

It's really simple. Go out tomorrow and buy three bottles of wine. Drink one; keep two. You've started a cellar.

The first thing to realize about owning a wine cellar is that it can be set up any place, from a room in your basement to a bedroom closet. It also can be any size that fits your needs—20 bottles or 2,000.

But the first step is to make that small start. Once you've done that, you can build your collection slowly and sensibly. The same rules for caring for it apply pretty much regardless of size.

The second step is to build some variety and backlog and to learn a little more about your tastes in the process. Many wine books will helpfully list a beginner's cellar of 50 bottles, and I suppose there are some people who begin collecting by simply going out and buying those. But they miss some education along the way.

Assuming that you're used to ordering a "glass of red wine" with your meal at a restaurant, you may not know about the different tastes of wine according to the grapes used, the area where they were grown, or the manner in which they were made into wine. The best way to learn these differences is to start by buying 20 bottles over the next month. Don't save any of these; they are strictly for drinking. All of these will be fairly inexpensive, and they probably won't be the tops in their categories.

However, they will tell you what you like. You might find the price and taste of a California Zinfandel to your taste and decide it will be your "everyday red" or "hamburger wine"—that is, the wine that you drink when you simply want wine with your meal. Another wine might become your "everyday white" or "chicken wine."

Some wines you might like occasionally; others not at all. You might also decide that you especially like the taste of wines made from Chardonnay grapes, so you'll start buying them from different wineries and regions. This becomes your area of specialization.

But let's not get too far ahead, and let's not pick those 20 out of the air.

A beginning list should provide you with a fairly good cross-section of what the market has to offer. First, whites: Muscadet, Gewürztraminer, Vouvray, Bordeaux white, Mâcon white, Soave, Moselle Kabinett, a California Chardonnay, Orvieto secco, and Sancerre. For reds: "Chantefleur," Petite Sirah, Côtes-du-Rhône, Médoc, Rioja, Cabernet Sauvignon, Bardolino, Bourgogne Passe-Tout-Grains, Beaujolais, Barbera, and Zinfandel.

This is obviously a very limited list, but it is a beginning. Except for the "Chantefleur," which is a specific brand, simply ask your wine merchant for a good bottle of Bardolino or whatever is in your price range. Incidentally, a good wine merchant is as valuable as a good stockbroker. No, more valuable, as a wine merchant knows the inside tips and can steer you toward bargains and sales—if he (or she) is a good merchant.

As you drink through these 20 or so wines, buy a few bottles or perhaps a case of those that you particularly like. With a little luck, you may end up with 20 or 30 bottles of wine suitable for a variety of occasions.

Which leads us to the third step. A good cellar should be able to take care of whatever needs you have, and it makes more sense to buy according to potential needs rather than by geography—so many wines from Napa Valley, so many from the Médoc, so many from the Rhine. For example, a person who has many formal dinners will have different wine needs than a person who does a lot of casual entertaining.

Following is such a listing of some wines for different occasions or levels of entertaining. As you build your collection of wines, you will gradually be stocking and re-stocking your cellar according to your lifestyle.

Everyday meals: Try to keep it at around $3 to $5 or less a bottle, and seek wines that have some range. Muscadet, Vouvray, Green Hungarian, Chilean Rieslings, California table whites and Soave are all good everyday whites. California table reds, Dão, Rioja, Egri Bikavér, California Barberas, cheaper Petite Sirahs and Zinfandels, and Chilean Cabernet Sauvignons are good red bargains.

Parties: If your guests are drinking glass after glass with assortments of hors d'oeuvre, then you might as well lay in a few jugs of California "burgundies" and "chablis." Anything else would be wasted.

Good meals: Try to stay with regional Bordeaux and lesser "châteaux," Châteauneuf-du-Pape, Chianti, California Cabernet Sauvignons and better Zinfandels, regional or village Burgundies for reds; Alsatian and California Rieslings, regional or village Burgundies, Bordeaux, lesser California Chardonnays, better Chenin Blancs and Sauvignon Blancs, and Mâcon in better years for whites.

133

Special meals: Your budget's the limit. For whites, the best of California Chardonnays, Burgundy, Bordeaux. For reds, the best of Médoc, California Cabernet Sauvignons, Côte Rôtie, Hermitage, Barolo, Burgundy. Merchants will be glad to point these out.

Celebrations: Sparkling wines, of course. A good non-vintage Champagne for $10 to $15; Schramsberg, Chandon, Korbel "champagnes" from California, and Sekt Trocken from Germany.

Before dinner: Something light and something to whet the appetite. Try a Rhine or Moselle Kabinett, a sparkling wine, a sherry or Madeira.

Dessert, after-dinner: Something sweet, such as a real Sauternes from France, a Moselle or Rhine Auslese, or a heavier sherry or Port.

Outdoors: Anything that can be chilled and that is light, such as Beaujolais or Bardolino for reds, any rosé, and Moselle and Rhine Kabinetts, Vouvrays, and Chenin Blancs for whites.

The point here is to be prepared for any occasion and to have extra depths in those categories you most use. For example, you may want only a bottle or two of a dessert wine and cases of everyday wine. At any rate, by the time you've finished this third step, you should have 50 to 100 bottles, and you will have a good basic cellar.

The fourth step is laying down wines, that is, buying wines now that will improve with age. Chiefly, but not exclusively, this means reds. Bordeaux, Burgundies, Côte Rôties and Hermitages from the Rhône Valley, Barolos from Italy, and some Cabernet Sauvignons and Zinfandels from California are prime examples of wines that may need aging.

But why should you do it? For one thing, by the time you have reached this point, you'll probably be so hooked on building your collection that no one could stop you from doing what eventually makes great cellars. But the main reasons are that, in theory, if you bought a wine made in 1975 when it came on the market (after oak aging) in 1978 and which will be at its peak in 1985, it was cheaper than it will be in 1985, you're sure that it's been properly stored, and, perhaps most important, it may not be available in 1985.

Following a sensible plan of laying down wines is a topic that can be explored later. For the moment, you might want to consult with your wine merchant about buying some 1976 California Cabernets, some 1975 Bordeaux, and some 1976 Burgundies. Unfortunately, most wine merchants do not stock a variety of vintages of the better Rhônes and Italian reds, so you often have to take (or leave) what's available.

Once you've reached this juncture, you may find a pattern evolving to your wine shopping. If you buy monthly, you may find that you'll need, say, 20 assorted bottles to replenish your stock, another half-dozen or so bottles of untried wines—new grape variety, new year, new label—and a bottle or two of a wine to lay down, occasionally splurging with a case to lay down.

Also, you'll notice that more frequent browsing will make you aware of changes in stock while the wine merchant becomes aware of you as a valued customer. You'll get the tip on when the next vintage of Bordeaux is due and what to look for. Perhaps, you'll even get a taste from a good bottle that has just been uncorked in the back room.

Finally, you'll be looking for bargains. Generally, these will be for current drinking as the merchant seeks to rid his shelves of wines that are passing their peaks and should be quickly consumed. For example, recently I have had excellent buys on a 1973 Dry Creek Zinfandel, a 1975 Delas Côte-du-Rhône, and 1973 Château Gloria.

Obviously, a few words should be said about how to store your wine. Perhaps, at some date, you may have special air-conditioned caves under your front lawn to accommodate

10,000 bottles, but a few simple rules for the present. One, store the wine on its side to keep the corks tight. Two, try to keep it cool (about 55 degrees is ideal), but above all don't store it where the temperature fluctuates wildly. Three, keep wine away from light, as light and heat age wine quickly. Four, keep it away from vibration, such as a refrigerator, which can seriously upset the wine. Five, normal humidity is fine, but too much is better than too little, which dries the corks.

As far as storage is concerned, racks that have separate niches for each bottle are fine but can get expensive with large collections. Bins are ideal to store cases of the same wine but not for assorted bottles, as it means you constantly have to shift the wine around to get what you need.

Now, we come full circle. You want to have your own cellar, but you aren't sure if it's necessary or desirable.

It definitely is. The best reason is that you have what you need when you need it. No more running out to the liquor store at 8 P.M. when unexpected guests arrive; no more drinking a rosé with steak.

There are other reasons. You can buy wine when it's a bargain or on sale. You can get a scarce wine that needs aging before it sells out. You can insure proper aging because you're doing it. It's a good way to learn about wine (although you should buy a basic "text" such as Frank Schoonmaker's *Encyclopedia of Wines* or Terry Robards' *New York Times Book of Wine* to help you along). Old wines need decanting, which means they can't be shaken as you rush home with a bottle from the corner store.

But most of all, keeping a cellar is romantic. Wine should be practical and a part of everyday life, but it also should be mysterious, fascinating, and full of lore. In our minds' eyes, it is only a small jump from our 100-bottle collections in reconverted rec rooms to the musty, centuries-old tasting rooms at Beaune with the light from the tallow candles glinting off the silver tasting cups.

Chapter Thirty-three

On keeping a wine log

RECENTLY some friends of mine were serving pre-dinner drinks and talking about wine—a subject in which they are only moderately interested—when the hostess asked if I would like to have the last few ounces of some Tokay Essence which they had purchased years earlier in London. The near-empty bottle was about to be tossed.

As Essence is a rare, legendary wine that could easily fetch a hundred dollars a bottle were one able to find it, my answer was definitely yes. The wine was superb, and I drove away that evening realizing that I may never again have the opportunity to taste this Hungarian delicacy.

Consequently, I doubt that I will ever forget the taste. Nevertheless, I quickly jotted down a page-long description in my wine journal where other interesting, if less regal, bottles are chronicled.

For many wine lovers, making such notes about what one drinks is as much a part of the wine life as smelling the cork of a newly opened bottle. Generally, this habit takes two forms: a cellar book or cellar log and a wine journal.

A wine journal is the simpler of the two. Whether it's a vest-pocket notebook that one carries to restaurants and on travels or a more formidable, bound book on the coffee table, a wine journal is a place to record your impressions of wines you drink that are not from your own cellar. One entry may be a wine tried in a restaurant that you simply want to note for later purchase. Another entry might be a prose poem to a romantic evening in which wine was only part of the charm.

A cellar log serves a different purpose: the recording of your purchases and how you "disposed" of them. As the French refer to a wine cellar as a *bibliothèque* or library, a term we have also adopted, your wine log might be considered a card catalogue. Indeed, some people do keep track of their wine on index cards.

More common are actual books in loose-leaf form, commercially printed or self-designed. Some people arrange their books by categories of wines, but a simpler way is to log wines chronologically as you buy them, putting a number in your book and a corresponding one linked on the label.

The first column in the log is generally the wine and vintage—"Scharzhofberger Spätlese 1975" or "Gallo Hearty Burgundy NV." Next you might have a column headed "region"—"The Saar" or "California," for example.

Other categories indicate the route the wine has taken in case you want to track down a bottle later. In my log, the heading is "Those Responsible," which covers *négociants*, shippers, *Weinguts,* bottlers, importers, exporters. This is helpful if you received a bottle as a gift or purchased it out of town and want your local merchant to try to buy more for you.

Which leads to another heading: "Purchasing Data" for when and where purchased, at what cost, in what quantity.

As mentioned, you might want a column which notes the bottle number. Thus, three years later, when you've consumed the wine, the number leads you back to the proper entry for comment.

Under "Comments," you can include a few words or sentences of description of the wine and the circumstances (meal, companions) of the drinking. For wines I drink regularly and which are fairly common, I may make no notation or simply a cursory one: "more acid than usual." The date consumed can also be logged here or under a separate heading.

Finally, you might consider a rating entry as a quick reference. Make up your own or use the common zero to 20 method. Or use letters of the alphabet if you're still thinking academically. (Would a wine that is not matured merit an "I" for incomplete?)

The wine and food journals often advertise cellar books that have places for pasting labels, but this is a cumbersome, space-consuming method, complicated by the fact that many producers use label glue that could endure The Flood and still not loosen.

If you want to take the time to make your own book, you can do so inexpensively by having a printing shop set the type for the column headings and pull you a proof. Paste the words in their proper place on a clean sheet of paper, and a photoduplicating firm can run heads off for a few dollars. A hole punch and an accounting-style binder finishes the job. If you have a flair for beautiful writing or calligraphy, you don't even have to bother with having type set. The black ink will duplicate just as well.

None of this will make the wine taste better, even if it's a Tokay Essence. But it might improve the memory of it as the years pass.

Chapter Thirty-four

Laying down wines

MORE than one wine lover has probably sat musing, over a glass of claret on a quiet evening, as to how his cellar is in many ways managed like a financial portfolio. The analogy is intriguing.

The easiest part is current drinking. As with a checking account, there are regular deposits—ten bottles or so monthly to be withdrawn in a few days' time as the occasion warrants. The account dips toward a deficit near month's end, and it's off to the wine merchant's to round up another deposit.

Future stock, like long-range investments and retirement plans, is a more difficult matter.

What châteaux or domaines represent the best investment this year? How long should they be kept to maturity? Should you gamble with wine futures, which, like futures in pork bellies, may turn out to be pigs-in-a-poke? How much will you need to tide you over in 1995? And how will you know when to capitalize on your investment?

Alas, there are no certainties in wine as there are none in

financial matters, and we Sylvia Porters of the wine trade can only give you general guidelines. If you take a bath . . . well, there are worse things than taking a dip in slightly over-the-hill Burgundy.

Of course, when talking about "laying down" wines, we are concentrating on a very small percentage of red ones. Most wines are to be drunk fresh, generally within three to five years of harvest, and any additional age will often result in vinegary or medicinal tastes.

Sticking with the table reds, for we need more of them in our cellar than we do dessert or fortified wines, the buyer should be concerned primarily with the kings and queens of France—Burgundies and Bordeaux—and the Cabernet Sauvignon of California. As your portfolio becomes more diversified, you will probably want to invest in Barolos and Brunellos di Montalcino of Italy, Hermitages and Côte Rôties (and possibly Cahors) from France, and some California Zinfandels. While the tastes of these wines vary considerably, all depend on tannin, a substance found in grape seeds and skins and in oak casks, for their long-livelihood.

To further simplify matters, let's concern our search for future stock to those wines with very good vintages that have recently come on market. The basic idea is to lay down only wines from great areas in great years as soon as they come on the market or even before, as in the case of "futures."

Why? Only great wines are worth the bother of tracking down and gambling on for the future, and then only in the best years. The reasons to buy them early are many, but three stand out: with a few exceptions, that's when they're cheapest to buy; many rare wines quickly go off the market; you can be sure they're aged properly in your own, and not someone else's, cellar.

The next concern is how long should we wait to capitalize on our investment? This question is almost as difficult as trying to decide, in advance, when to sell your blue-chip stocks. But there are some rules. Presuming we're talking about great years, most red wines worthy of laying down should peak in five to ten years and possibly make great drinking for another ten before fading.

Some Bordeaux over 100 years old are still good, but wines made today are vinified to reach their peak much sooner. Obviously, not all wines from a superior geographic area are equal. As a rule, the greater vineyards will last longer to peak. A Bordeaux such as Château La Tour de By may be ready in five, while a Château Mouton-Rothschild may take fifteen years. The Southern European wines such as Barolo, Hermitage, and Côte Rôtie would be safer at ten years, perhaps twenty years for a Brunello.

So how do you reduce these risks? By doing as an investor would—rely on your own knowledge and that of an expert. Before most wine buyers get within two years of seeing a Bordeaux on their merchants' shelves, the wine experts who write columns and publish newsletters have already tasted much of the château wine in the cask. (There is a two to four year lag between harvest and buying, as the wine ages in oak casks.) These tastings, coupled with their knowledge of the weather, will give them an idea of how good the vintage is and how long it might last. The word slips out only months after the harvest: such-and-such vintage is great, mediocre, or lousy. This is when you start to make your plans.

However, just as with the stock market, experts need not have all the fun. You should begin to develop your own tastes and judgments to supplement what you read. For example, perhaps you decide you want to buy a lesser Bordeaux—a "petit château"—which may cost around a third or less of what the better châteaux will command.

First, buy one bottle and taste it. What are you looking for? Many things as you learn, but first concentrate on tannin and fruit. Tannin can be described as a harsh, but not unpleasant, taste that tends to pucker the mouth, much as a pecan shell would, around the gum line. If the wine is full and tannic, then it should age well. Additionally, there should also be some hints of fruitiness—otherwise, there's no need to lay down the wine in the first place. (If the wine tastes delicious now, with little tannin, buy a case, but don't save it as it will probably not improve.)

As a further step, artificially age the wine by leaving some in the glass for an hour or so. If the wine is still harsh, but is improving in taste, then you know you will have wine worth aging. This will also give you a hint of the mature taste of the wine. If it becomes weak or acidy, why gamble? Having determined that the wine will age (tannin) and is worth aging (fruit), commence your buying.

The next step is to sample a bottle in three or so years, always keeping an eye on the experts' opinions of the general vintage. Does the wine have a brownish tinge around the edge as you swirl it in the glass? If so, it may be starting to decline. How is the tannin? Compare the taste now with your notes from the previous tasting. Little by little you begin to learn, making notes on the amount of glycerin present, the finish, and so on. By the time you get to the third or fourth bottle, the wine may be at its peak and you will have learned considerably.

Not that one can ever get smug. The late Frank Schoonmaker, one of the most respected American tasters, wrote in his early appraisal of the 1973 Burgundy vintage that the wine would not peak for about ten years. His first tastes were deceiving, however, as that very fine vintage matured quickly like Lolita.

The final consideration for investing in wine also has a money parallel: how much of what will I need, and when? Again, one man's poverty is another's richness. But let me suggest a modest system.

First you have to determine how many bottles of fine wine you will normally need. For example, if you normally have a fancy dinner for yourself or for guests twice a month, that means you will need a minimum of 24 bottles, or two cases, annually. Throw in another case if you entertain, or expect to frequently—36 bottles total. Figure half of the time you will probably have a dinner that calls for red wine, and half for white. *Voilà*. You need about 18 bottles of very good red wine a year, not counting your everyday drinking.

Since good years in the vineyards cannot be anticipated, how will you know how much to buy in a good year now to insure your 18 bottles later? One way is to play the averages. In the five-year period from 1970 to 1974, there were seven very good to excellent years total in Bordeaux, Burgundy, and Northern California. This record appears to be fairly average for a five-year period. Consequently, if you had purchased one case of each superior vintage in the three separate areas, you would have stored seven cases—or 84 bottles—almost your desired 18 bottles per year. You can work out the multiples according to your drinking patterns.

Personally, I would recommend buying two cases from each outstanding vintage, one average château or vineyard and one superior one, depending on your budget.

If you buy a case of all the same wine, it is easier to track its maturity. However, it is enjoyable to buy individual bottles of the same vintages for comparative tastings at a later date. Obviously, you can also weight your buying toward a certain area, say, if you prefer Bordeaux over Burgundy.

A few stores will offer you a risky investment which you might want to try, and that is wine futures. Essentially, you are buying the vintage and the château or domaine on their reputations because you purchase the wine at its cheapest before the wine merchant actually has it on hand and before you have the opportunity to taste it.

If you become conscientious in your reading and drinking, you can reduce the gamble, as many wine writers, particularly those who do newsletters, may preview the same wines you may be considering buying. So, futures become the biggest risk in our wine cellar/financial portfolio analogy.

However, there is one area where the analogy does not hold up. If your wine matures well and becomes valuable, the Internal Revenue Service has not yet come up with a way of taxing these delicious dividends.

Chapter Thirty-five

How to rate wines

THE other day, some of us were sitting around discussing the movie *10*, which takes its name from the old masculine game of rating the physical beauty of a woman on a scale of zero to ten.

"If Bo Derek is a ten," one fellow ventured, "then Julie Andrews must be an 11."

This was not stated simply as a difference of opinion with the hero's (Dudley Moore) score card, but it was an argument against the nature of the system itself.

Let me explain. Rating women is essentially a boys' game, no matter what their ages. And when you're in prep school, there is a tendency to make a science out of what is essentially a game. My fuzzy-faced cronies and I used to watch girls play intramural basketball, and we would rate them so many points on legs, so many on breasts (we could only guess), so much on face, and so on.

But eventually some of us rebelled against the system. A tallying of the parts, we argued, did not justify the sum total.

Or as my movie-going friend observed, Bo Derek may indeed rate a ten if determined category by category. But as a sexy-looking woman totally, he would prefer Julie Andrews.

We get into much the same argument when we talk about rating wines. Some people like to make it as scientific as possible; others—including myself—believe rating cannot be, or at least should not be, scientific, but rather emotional and subjective.

Wines are rated at two points. The first is the vintage itself. Some, like the late Frank Schoonmaker, rated vintages on a scale of zero to 20.

The second rating is of individual bottles of wine. The rating may be done by a panel assembled by a wine writer, who then passes on a numerical collective judgment to her readers. It may be done during formal competition, say the Los Angeles County Fair.

Because rating for competitive reasons is universal, many experts seek a system that is uniform and which can be uniformly communicated to drinkers who have criteria for interpreting. It is here, I fear, that we get into the same trouble that tripped up Dudley Moore.

Take the most popular of rating systems, the Amerine Method. The credentials, knowledge, and contributions of Professor Maynard Amerine of the University of California at Davis are impeccable. But I still don't like his system.

Amerine perfection is 20 points, which is calculated according to appearance (two), color (two), aroma and bouquet (four), vinegary (the absence thereof, rating two), total acidity (two), sweetness (correctness, rating one), flavor (two), body (one), bitterness and astringency (two), and general quality (two).

I admit the system is flexible according to types of wine, and I admit that some of my personal preferences are arguable. For example, I know a winemaker will make some preliminary decisions about his wine according to its color, but to add or subtract points according to color seems too esoteric to me. Our taste/smell sensations are chemically linked to each other, so neither can be ignored in judging how a wine tastes, which is the point after all, and not its looks.

Beyond this, I have several objections to the nature of the system itself.

One, theoretically a Vouvray could rate 20, and a Trockenbeerenauslese could rate 20. The best Vouvray cannot compare with the best Trock, and the Amerine system as interpreted does not easily allow for inter-varietal rating; it would be difficult for any scientific system to do so.

Two, sometimes a particular quality is so outstanding that it can almost make a bottle great even if some other characteristics are average. Weighted systems do not recognize this.

Third, it is our nature to judge wines by almost undefinable qualities—aroma, complexity of taste, finish, aftertaste, flaws—which considered together tell us how well we liked the wine, if we like it at all.

We can best do this, I believe, by considering the parts as a whole and not by separating them and then adding them up after the tasting experience.

Like many people, I have my own system to communicate with myself, but it, like others, could easily be communicated to anyone else. I rate zero to 100 because it gives me great flexibility. Ninety-five to 100 is "rare," those absolutely unbelievable, seldom-seen wines that can be extremely difficult to describe because everything is so harmoniously integrated. Ninety to 94 is "exceptional"; 85 to 89, "very good" or "delicious"; and so on.

After having mulled over a wine and evaluated its total impact, I can easily assign it to one of my categories and then I can further give it a number—say from 80 to 84—within that category.

Of course, you may still give Bo Derek a ten even if you use a subjective, and not a semi-scientific, rating system. The same with a seductive Montrachet. That is the comforting joy of wine.

Chapter Thirty-six

Wine gadgets

SAY it's getting close to Father's Day, and if Ol' Dad has a wine cellar, you might be tempted to buy him something that relates to his hobby.

Wine is probably the best gift, and a case of Bordeaux would surely be appreciated now and over the next few years. Then there are always some interesting new wine books out, such as the one you're reading.

But there is always cellar paraphernalia, either modern or antique, and such gadgetry can be appreciated by wine lovers who normally put their money into wine, not the accoutrements.

There is no need to waste money on an item that will never be used, however, or, worse, should never be used. What, then, is helpful in the cellar?

An unglamorous gift, but one I wish someone would buy me, is wine racks. There never seem to be enough wine racks. Check the old man's cellar and see if there are cases of wine resting on their sides or individual bottles stacked up in a corner. If so, there's your gift. The best racks are space-efficient and inexpensive. I particularly like the collapsible, wavy-metal ones that are often used, and sold, in liquor stores in case multiples such as 36 or 48 bottles.

A cellar book is another useful gift, particularly if Dad doesn't have one or if his current one is about used up. Again, efficiency counts—lots of pages and flexibility of format.

There is a whole series of items related to opening and decanting wine bottles. Anyone who drinks wine and doesn't have a fetish for metal caps probably has a useful corkscrew, but a second one is nice to have around. A few tips: best are the double-action (twin screw knobs), the screwpull coated screw, the wine waiter's (corkscrew with knife), and the Ah So type (a handle with two metal prongs). The kind with lever arms sometimes requires three hands. The screw itself should be hollow, sufficiently wide, with rounded, not cutting, edges.

Unless you drink vintage Port or older red table wines, you will seldom have to seriously decant—that is, decant for the purpose of getting rid of sediment. Experts argue over the best way to decant—with the sediment on the side of the bottle (as it would be when you took it from the rack or bin) or in the bottom (as it would be if you let it sit upright for a day or so). I belong to the latter school, believing more sediment is kept in the bottle, not the glass, in that manner.

Therefore, I am not too hot on wine baskets or cradles that keep the sediment on the side. Those who do use them for decanting place the bottle of wine in the basket before uncorking and pour the wine into a decanter through a funnel with a light (candle) behind the bottle in order to see that no mud gets through. In no case should the wine basket be brought to the table, as sediment almost always gets into your glass when you pour that way.

A good glass or silver funnel, slightly curved at the bottom to let the wine gently trickle down the sides of the decanter, is an excellent, inexpensive gift.

Decanters themselves are pretty and show a wine off well. Some people decant all wines strictly for this reason, never bringing a bottle to the table. The only question here is your own taste in crystal and how much you care to spend.

Tastevins are those shallow little silver cups that look like bumpy ashtrays at the end of a chain. If you are tasting a lot of wines, as a cellarmaster at a winery would be, they are helpful. Let Dad have one if he wants, anyway, but don't let him dangle it against his white shirt after sampling.

Ice buckets, particularly silver and elaborate glass ones, are also pretty, but they are generally more trouble than they're worth. A restaurant may need one to quickly chill a wine, but your refrigerator is much more efficient. Wine that is already chilled will lose some of its bouquet if allowed to wallow too long in a freezing bucket, and you'll get water marks on your table, anyway. The only time I use an ice bucket is for a backyard picnic on a hot summer day, and a lot of that is psychological.

Those chemical wine chillers are even more worthless. You really shouldn't try to chill a wine in a few minutes, but if you have to in an emergency, use a lesser white wine and chill it in the freezer. At least the freezer will uniformly cool the bottle, while one of those thermal gadgets leaves the neck sticking out unchilled. Guess where the first glass of wine comes from.

Wine bricks use the thermos bottle principle, keeping white wines cold and red ones at moderate cellar temperatures. They do no real harm, but Dad really won't need one unless he drinks very slowly in an ice house or a sauna. Normally, your wine will stay at a reasonable temperature throughout a meal without any gadgetry.

Coasters to set wine in—generally pewter or silver with a cork liner—are essential, and an extra one or two can be used during a wine party.

Chapter Thirty-seven

What glass for what wine

THE classic remarks on what are the requirements of a wine glass were delivered by wine expert and merchant, Julius Wile.

"It shouldn't leak," he said.

True enough, but my youthful wine-drinking buddies in West Virginia thought even the use of a glass was a bit effete and a waste of pouring time, preferring instead to drink directly from the bottle encased in a brown paper bag or poke.

Of course, there is a complex etiquette of wine glasses rooted partly in tradition and partly in reason. As far as the latter is concerned, the evolution of the wine glass over hundreds of years has progressed beyond the requirement that it not leak.

The first of these evolutionary improvements is the stem. True, there are Paris cafés where wine is drunk from a squat tumbler, which the department stores that sell them would have you believe is the way that the true French wine drinkers do it. Actually, it only shows that France has its share of unsophisticated drinkers. But back to the stem: it keeps your fingerprints off the bowl of the glass, and hence gives an unimpaired view of the wine; it allows you to keep the wine at the temperature served without being warmed by sweaty fingers and palms; it allows you to better swirl the wine in the bowl to release aromas.

The bowl itself should be large and tapered inward toward the top, but with no lip. Why this shape? First, the bowl should be large enough to allow a reasonable portion to be held without filling the glass more than halfway, thus allowing the rest of the bowl to be engulfed by the aroma of the wine. Additionally, the extra space allows for swirling, which releases the smells and lets a strong red breathe a bit. The tapering toward the top also allows for swirling to be contained without spilling and helps hold in the smells for you to sniff.

As long as you have a set of glasses which have the proper stem and bowl standards, you really don't need anything else. But if you enjoy good crystal and like to dress up a table, there are a number of traditional glasses you might want to consider for variety.

The basic shape is the tulip, of which there are many varieties. The tulip has a tapered bottom balanced by a tapered top with the rim turning slightly inward. Some people use this as the all-purpose glass.

Also familiar, and a bit controversial, is the Burgundy bowl or *balon*, sometimes called a balloon glass for its size. This is a larger, more open glass, although it does come in a bit at the top. Frankly, some people are embarrassed because of its size, but I find it useful with an assertive red that doesn't need to be coaxed too much but does need to be mellowed by airing the largest possible surface.

Although many drink Bordeaux from a tulip, the classic Claret glass is U-shaped, coming in more sharply at the bottom than does the tulip. The tulip, Burgundy bowl, and Claret glass are the primary red glasses, although their use is not restricted to reds.

Champagne and other sparkling wines are generally served in a tulip, a coupe, or a flute. The Champenois themselves prefer an elongated tulip which allows the bubbles to climb upward, upward in beautiful flight. Americans like the saucer-shaped coupe, an utterly worthless glass whose only distinction is being shaped after Marie Antoinette's or Helen of Troy's breast, depending on your preference in legends. The flute is my favorite. Although it does not allow swirling, as its elegant elongation has no proper bowl and opens slightly outward, it does allow for maximum display of wine and bubbles. Hollow-stemmed glasses are a bit more difficult to keep sanitary, however.

The Northern whites from the Loire, Alsace, and Germany are served in more elaborate colored and faceted glasses. For a tasting, clear glass gives a better evaluation of the wine, but these traditional shapes can show off the wines adequately and decorate the table. The Anjou glass is more flat-bottomed with steep shoulders. Alsatian glasses are often green-stemmed.

There is a myriad of regional distinctions within the German glasses, but, generally, the Rhine glasses have knobby, often brown stems, but not as knobby as the Franken, which looks as though it were turned on a lathe. Mosel-Saar-Ruwer glasses often feature etched or cut-glass bowls. If you want to pay $20–$40 a stem, there are some beautiful pastel bowls with colored glass in antique stores.

Dessert wines are often shown off in long-stemmed glasses with smaller bowls (since you drink less of these). Sherry, dessert or otherwise, is often served in a small, but elongated, tulip called a *copita*.

California? There are no regional shapes there, but I'm sure someone will eventually create an instant tradition.

After all, if a glass could be designed after Marie Antoinette's breast, think what could be done for wine lovers if someone wanted to immortalize some of the more prominent Hollywood starlets.

Chapter Thirty-eight

Notes on bottles

SOME time ago, in a Pasadena wine store, I ran across Sweet Nancy.

Sweet Nancy, of course, is the name of a dessert wine made from botrysized grapes from the property of Eli Callaway. I had been anxious to try Sweet Nancy, but I had always been frightened away by her price tag, which runs into double digits. Fortunately for me, Sweet Nancy was stocked in half-bottles at the store—still expensive at that time at $6, but located at a spot on my mental chart where the desire curve and cost line are in proximity.

Sweet Nancy is not an oddity—California dessert wines have become the rage—nor is the practice of wineries selling half-bottles. In recent months I have been attracted to buys of a regional Sauternes, a Delas Côtes-du-Rhône, and Mondavi Cabernet Sauvignon, all in halves.

Perhaps we have been too rash in summarily dismissing the packaging—in this case, bottles—as completely unrelated to the product. Generally, there is a method, and a reason, to why bottles are the way they are.

This is especially true of the half, which seems to be a barometer of our social times. Inflation bothering you? What better way than first trying a half bottle to see if you really like a wine. Divorced or single or, as is the case with my wife and me, your spouse is often out of town on business? A half makes the perfect companion to a meal, enough to whet the appetite but not enough to bring an early end to the evening. Additionally, a half is the right size for a dessert wine—enough to handle a dinner party of four to eight.

However, if you plan to buy in large lots for your cellar (remembering that there are 24 bottles to the case), don't keep the halves on the shelf as long as you would regular-sized bottles. The smaller the container, the quicker the wine ages.

If halves (often called "tenths"—half of a "fifth"—by merchants) have their place in the scheme of drinking, so do larger bottles. With table wines, that means magnums (2 bottles), double magnums (4), jeroboams (6), and imperials (8). Champagne is a bit more confusing. Magnum still means 2 bottles, but jeroboam is 4. Up the line: rehoboam (6), methuselah (8), salmanazar (12), balthazar (16), and nebuchadnezzar (20), which is enough wine to make anyone think he is the king of Babylon.

In most cases, magnums are all you'll have special use for. Many Bordeaux are available in these two-bottle sizes, and I have laid down some magnums of fine 1975 Médocs with the anticipation of enjoying them at dinner parties for four—for which magnums are ideally suited—in the late 1980s. Of course, you could simply set out two regular bottles of the same wine, but, over the long haul of cellaring, there can be a difference in how each bottle fares. Additionally, you only have to decant once with a magnum.

If you're new to wine buying, or if you never paid too much attention to bottles, you might not know that there is some reason to the variety of shapes and colors. The most ready example stems from the fact that red wine is generally aged in the bottle, while most whites are generally consumed within a year after bottling. Hence red wines are almost always in dark green or brown bottles, as the colored glass keeps out light which can age a wine too quickly. Since white wine does not need this protection, most of them are in lighter colored bottles or even in clear, colorless bottles.

There is less reason for the evolution of bottle shapes and colors according to region (and there is little reason to know what bottle is from what region, unless you're too lazy to read the label). Most German bottles are long and tapered— green for Mosel-Saar-Ruwer and brown for Rhine. Alsace, once a part of Germany, has green bottles, slightly longer than the German bottles. An exception to the tapered class is the Franconian *bocksbeutel* which looks something like a Mateus bottle and has an absolutely foul translation.

Bordeaux wines are in bottles whose shoulders curve in sharply at the neck, dark green for red, clear glass for white. Chianti bottles, except for the cheaper *fiasco* (straw-covered, squat bottles), and Rioja bottles are generally similar to Bordeaux.

Burgundy has sloped shoulders, and both red and white come in green bottles. Loire bottles also have sloped shoulders, but are slightly more tapered than Burgundies. Rhône and Barolo bottles are similar to Burgundy, with the latter being a little heavier in design. Most Beaujolais comes in Burgundy bottles, technically correct anyway, although some come in "pots" which have huge, bulging shoulders.

California wines have no traditional shapes or colors, except that Cabernet Sauvignon naturally comes in a Bordeaux bottle, Pinot Noir in a Burgundy bottle, and so on.

But don't feel sorry for the Californians. Some of the wineries have decided to dispense with the bottle altogether. Ever see those wine-in-a-glass, flipover plastic containers at the checkout counter?

And then there's the wine in a box put out by Geyser Peak in its Summit brand. The box has a plastic bladder inside with a nozzle for dispensing. It doesn't make the wine taste any better, but you don't lose a drop when you're pouring in the back-of-the-bus, commuter wine party.

PART SIX
Deviations from the Norm

Chapter Thirty-nine

Aperitif wines

NOT long ago, a business colleague and I had finished a long day of work and were relaxing before dinner on the verandah of the White Cliffs Hotel in Dover, watching the late afternoon sun glint off the rippled waters on the Channel.

Now, a little something to drink. A fino sherry for me, a Martini for him. The French bartender carefully measured a jigger of gin into a tall glass and proceeded to fill the glass to the brim with dry Vermouth. My friend was so horrified he could not protest. The bartender turned to another customer, no doubt happy that he had been so generous with his Vermouth.

The incident shows well the difference between the traditional European idea of a before-dinner drink—something to whet the appetite—and the American idea of a before-dinner drink—something to ease the day's mental and physical burdens.

I admit to going back and forth between the two, depending

upon my mood, but there is no doubt that the amount of alcohol in most cocktails will dull, rather than tantalize, the tastebuds. For that reason the ideal before-dinner drink is light and lively: not too sweet, not too heavy, not too potent. Just enough to stir up the gastric juices.

A glass of white wine from the bar generally serves that purpose, but it would be a mistake to think that the world of aperitifs and appetizer wines ends there.

Among the more popular appetizer wines in Europe are the aromatics, wines to which some herb or other flavorings have been added. Most familiar with Americans is Dubonnet, a brand name, which comes in red (slightly sweet) and white (drier), the former being the most popular. Both have bitters and quinine added, and both are now manufactured in the United States as well as France, home of the original concoction.

Other brand-name aromatics which you might want to try, either chilled, on the rocks, or with a splash of soda, are Byrrh and St. Raphael (brandy and quinine added) and Lillet (brandy but no quinine).

In some ways Vermouths are more aromatics than wine in that they are tinkered with and added to and pasteurized to the point that the grape origin is hardly recognized. Few Americans drink Vermouth straight, preferring the dry, white, "French" vermouth for Martinis and Gibsons and the red, sweeter, "Italian" version for Manhattans. Vermouths vary according to herbs added, but all in theory have worm-wood flower as a common ingredient.

Then there are the drinks known as bitters, of which Campari and Punt e Mes are probably the most noteworthy.

What the British refer to as "cups"—drinks in which wine and other liquids are mixed, a wine cocktail if you will—are also gaining some acceptance in the United States. Most popular is Kir, not a favorite of mine, where a few drops of crème de cassis or blackcurrant are added to white wine, traditionally a white Burgundy. Considering the prices of even lesser white Burgundies, the American habit of using any jug white is at least economically sound.

Other cups include slightly sweet German whites with soda, ambrosia (orange juice and sparkling wine, a brunch alternative to the Bloody Mary), and Pimm's Cup (a pre-mixed proprietary brand).

My preference for a before-dinner drink is a dry sherry or Madeira. Don't make the mistake of getting a sweet, dessert version. It will kill the appetite instead of stimulating it. With sherries, ask for a fino, a pale dry, or a Manzanilla (actually a neighbor of the true Spanish sherries of Jerez). I am fond of El Tio Pepe, a popular brand.

The dry Madeiras are called *sercial*, and one of my favorites in price and taste is a sercial called Rainwater Madeira

The bubbles in Champagne and other sparkling wines are an ideal aid to appetite, providing the wine is not too sweet, as with many of the Italian spumantes, or too fruity, as is the case of the New York State wines. If you didn't get around to them during New Year's, try the better California sparkling wines, such as Kornell, Schramsberg, Chandon, Mirrasou, and Korbel.

Of course, there isn't anything wrong with the now-common glass of white. If you're planning a meal, try the non-sparkling wines of Champagne, called Côteaux Champenois, which are now reaching the U.S. in some volume. The Canard Duchène label is a favorite of mine.

As a matter of fact, the whole northern tier of France makes good appetizer wines, the Loire Valley being especially blessed with its Sancerres, Pouilly Fumés, and Muscadets. I personally find Chablis a bit too crisp for a sipping wine, preferring it with seafood, but many people like to start with a glass.

If you're a confirmed double Martini drinker and still don't know if you can cope with all this lightness, be like our French bartender. Throw in a splash of gin until you get the hang of it.

Chapter Forty

Well-seasoned wines

A writer friend of mine once published a satire on the sometimes overdramatized ritual of tasting a wine in a restaurant. In the article, he warned the uninitiated that it was necessary to knowingly pass judgment on the small amount poured by the waiter "or he won't let you have any more to drink."

"And it is not enough," he further wrote, "to scowl and mutter, 'Needs more salt.'"

Of course, the idea of adding salt, or pepper for that matter, to wine seems ludicrous to us. And it is. Yet while there is a grain of salt in my friend's barbs, there is also a grain of truth in them, for the practice of "seasoning" wines is as old—and new—as seasoning your steak, sole, or Big Mac.

It might surprise the sipper of sweet Vermouth or the swiller of Martinis that they are drinking as many herbs and spices as covers a chicken that has run the gantlet at Colonel Sanders. In fact, Vermouth has so many herbs that it would be right at home on the shelves of a health food store.

The whole matter of seasoning wines developed with ancient winemakers who weren't as fussy as we are and who didn't have to worry about the label requirements of the Treasury Department.

If a wine tasted a bit sour, then a reasoning Roman would stir in a dollop of honey. If some of the taste of the pine resin used to seal the amphorae showed up in the chalice, then the Greeks figured that was the way the wine poured.

As a group, we call these grape wines which have had something added to improve or change the taste aromatic or flavored wines. They should not be confused with fruit wines—such as apple or cherry—or other similar wines which use something other than grapes to provide the sugar for fermentation.

Chief among these aromatics are the Vermouths, used throughout the world as aperitifs and mixers, particularly dry Vermouth in Martinis.

Vermouth is the corruption of the German word for wormwood, the near lethal ingredient in absinthe. Both sweet and dry were developed independently in the late 1700s, so they are not really as old as many other aromatic concoctions. First to come, from northern Italy, was the bittersweet red or Italian Vermouth. A few years later a Frenchman derived a Vermouth from the white grapes of the Midi, inventing the drier or French Vermouth.

Today both dry and sweet Vermouths are made in both countries, and elsewhere, so the distinction is of historical rather than current consideration.

By French law, a Vermouth must be at least 80 percent wine, allowing for a generous addition of alcohol and sugar. Generally this added *vin de liqueur* or *mistelle* is used to soften the wine.

Then comes the kinky part. Proprietary blends of herbs and spices are steeped in the wine to give it its distinctive aroma. What herbs? Try camomile. Or cinnamon, cloves, nutmeg, coriander—perhaps as many as two or three dozen different varieties may be added to the basic wine in a sort of Scarborough Fair parade. Then brandy is added to further increase the alcohol content.

Dubonnet—recently the rage of the chic midtown restaurant crowd—represents another category of aromatic wines, those that have quinine in them. As with Vermouth, the basic color may be white or red, again depending on the type of grapes used.

The quinine wines—or *quinquinas*—were invented as sort of medicinal wines. Because Europeans going off to colonize the world often exchanged civilized diseases such as smallpox for uncivilized diseases such as malaria, quinine was added to their stores of wines to stave off the tropical sicknesses.

As humans can grow used to almost anything, including medicine, quinine wines caught on, particularly in Southern Europe, and are today a principal aperitif of the region. Although Dubonnet may rest easily on palates of some beginners, many Americans first tasting other quinquinas may wonder if malaria wasn't preferable.

In addition to Dubonnet, other quinine wines include such proprietary brands as Punt e Mes, Lillet, Byrrh, and St. Raphael. Try them at least once so that you'll know what you're missing.

One aromatic wine that I particularly like is a northern one—May Wine from Germany—which to me signals the coming of spring which means I consume only about a bottle per year. But what a nice bottle. The primary flavoring in May Wine, which is light and fairly dry, is the herb woodruff. Going with tradition, I pour a generous amount of May Wine in one of those saucer glasses or coupes that most people drink Champagne out of (but shouldn't) and add fresh strawberries. After I've eaten and drunk my way through two or three glasses, then I'm ready for summer.

There are other aromatic wines, but let's finish with one of the more celebrated and unusual ones—retsina.

To say that retsina is an acquired taste may be somewhat of an understatement. The wine tastes of tar, pitch, or turpentine because resin is added to the wine—knowingly. Amphorae are no longer the vogue, even in Greece, so it is no longer a question of accident.

Introducing someone to retsina and ouzo, a licorice- or anise-flavored liquor, at a Greek or Middle Eastern restaurant is the dining equivalent of fraternity hazing.

Still, there is something to be said about retsina—what other wine could you want to consume with stuffed grape leaves? In view of my friend's comments on restaurant etiquette perhaps it's understandable that there is no tasting ritual involved when a glass of an aperitif—which most aromatic wines are—is served.

What wine waiter could tolerate the criticism, "Needs more paprika."

Chapter Forty-one

White wines from red grapes

THE bird's eye has flown the frozen vegetable counter and landed in the wine merchant's racks. Which is to say there is yet another line of wines being made in California—*oeil de perdrix* or eye of the partridge.

Eye of the partridge is an almost forgotten example of *blanc de noirs* or white wines made from black grapes. There are different gradations from the *blanc de noirs* of Champagne, in which the sparkling wine is almost clear, to *vin gris*, which has just a touch of gray-like pigmentation, to rosé, which is like a light red wine in some cases. Eye of the partridge falls in about the middle of this range—a light copper-to-apricot-hued wine which obviously reminded Frenchmen of the color of a partridge's eye.

Why this sudden interest in white or pale wine from red grapes? There are several reasons. First, California winemakers are notorious experimenters who will not rest until they have mastered and marketed every type of grape wine ever made. Second, American drinkers are essentially light-wine lovers, hence the popularity of rosés and whites. Third, California grape growers misread popular trends in the boom of the early 1970s and overplanted black grapes, especially Cabernet Sauvignon. As a result, there was actually a shortage of California whites in many East Coast states for a time during the late 1970s. Thus, the rush to get out all white wine possible, even if it meant making it from black grapes. After the "emergency" was over, the wines stayed around as their popularity had grown.

The whole process of making white from black is an interesting one, sometimes more interesting than the wines that result. Most grapes have no pigmentation in the juice (those that do are called *teinturiers* and are used primarily for coloring), as pigmentation is largely in the skins. If the juice is immediately separated from the black skins, it is largely indistinguishable in color from juice from white grapes.

In Champagne, for example, almost three quarters of the vineyards are planted in Pinot Noir and only one quarter in Chardonnay. Champagne can be made either totally from black grapes or totally from white grapes, although generally it is made from a mixture. The clarity of juice from the Pinot Noir is achieved by crushing and pressing at the same time, instead of by the normal two-step process. Thus the juice has only momentary contact with the skins. A *vin gris* has only slightly more exposure.

At the other end of the spectrum are the rosés. Rosés are fun to drink but not to be seriously considered, although this was not always the case. Once there was almost no red wine as such, as the process of the black skins remaining with the juice during fermentation was virtually unknown until the 1700s. Before this, Burgundy built its reputation on rosés.

August Sebastiani is responsible for reawakening interest in the lightly colored eye of the partridge wines a few years back, although he called his "eye of the swan." He apparently has no partridges in his aviary. His is a good wine to illustrate the merits—and lack of them—of the genre.

Sebastiani Eye of the Swan generally has a lemony color and a slightly acid, gamey nose that is characteristic of the Pinot Noir from which it and most other eye of the partridge wines are made. (Pinot Noir is an extremely adaptable grape—excellent strong Burgundies, whistle-light Champagnes, fruity rosés.) It is a delightful wine, very drinkable. It has a good balance between citrus and a "bitters" or soda-water taste that most *blanc de noirs* have as a result of the slight dose of tannin from the skins. It has substance, a slight gaminess, and what seems like a hint of oak.

Less successful, but more colorful, has been Caymus Vineyards Oeil de Perdrix, an extremely beautiful apricot-pink wine. At times it lacks fruitiness and substance and is short on foretaste. The bitters finish is pronounced and pleasant, but there has been little else to recommend it. Perhaps one could keep a bottle for aesthetic reasons and sip it as an aperitif.

More in the *vin gris* category are the white wines made from the Zinfandel, a black grape. The best I have tasted is Enz White Zinfandel 1977, made in Hollister in the San Benito Valley. It had a lovely foretaste, followed by sweetish glycerine taste, in turn replaced by a soda tartness at the finish. My only regret was in buying just one half-bottle at a roadside shop near Salinas.

Chapter Forty-two

Fruit wines

OFTEN we compare the taste of certain wine to fruits other than grapes.

For example, a mellow Moselle Auslese might be said to have the nectary aroma and taste of ripe peaches.

A good Cabernet Sauvignon is often given the attributes of currants.

And a dark, earthy red Rhône such as a Côte Rôtie often has a finish that reminds one of the last, lingering, stony taste of a dark cherry.

Yet most wine drinkers scorn a wine that tastes like peaches or cherries—if it is actually made from peaches or cherries. "Fruit" wines (as though a grape were anything else) are considered about as unclassy as you can get.

There are logical reasons for this snobbish attitude. For one thing, no fruit is as naturally suited to making wine as are grapes, and certainly none blends as well with food or has the range of taste possibilities. Second, many fruit wines are poorly made—generally too heavy and too sweet. Finally, most of the pop wines, such as Boone's Farm apple wine, are

173

made from fruits other than grapes, and who wants to drink what teenagers drink?

Still, we can be too stodgy about the matter.

A friend of mine a few years ago gave me a bottle of cherry wine issued by a new Pennsylvania winery, Country Creek of Telford. Not too long afterward, we were entertaining friends with a Sunday afternoon wine buffet, and I placed the Country Creek cherry wine with the dozen or so other wines for the eaters to choose from.

Even the most purple-blooded wine drinkers were delighted.

The chilled wine was fruity but not sweet and had a tart, stony finish with just a hint of sulphur, which, surprisingly, seemed to be a positive element. The wine went well as an aperitif and as accompaniment to baked ham.

So, if you're the adventuresome sort, or if spring makes you want to try something new, I urge you to sample a fruit wine or two, not only as a curiosity but as a class of wines that has a legitimate place in the spectrum of alcoholic beverages.

First, a few words about fruit wines as a group.

Fruit wines are generally made in areas where wine-quality grapes cannot be easily grown. Most American fruit wines are made outside of California, for example, although the Los Angeles County Fair has competition for berry wines just as surely as it has prizes for Cabernets.

It is not surprising that Pennsylvania, which has acres of orchard land, makes a number of good cherry and apple wines. Places like Michigan, Ohio, and Missouri are also hotbeds of fruit fermentation.

Nor are fruit wines strictly an American phenomenon. Most areas of northern France are not prime vineyard areas, and fruit wines are prevalent in the countryside. In Normandy, apple wines are made into an apple brandy which is known to the world as Calvados.

There are problems that are common to fruit wines. One

is that many fruits have a high acid, low sugar concentration, and, without additives, would make acidy, unstable, low-alcohol wines. For that reason, sugar is often added. In better growing areas, grapes less frequently have this problem.

Some home winemakers often carry the sugaring, or chaptalizing, to an extreme, with the result that many home fruit wines are as cloying as cough syrup. Still, I have a friend who makes a delicious, hearty elderberry wine that is to fruit wines what a robust Zinfandel is to grape wines.

You might have difficulty finding an elderberry wine on your merchant's shelves, however, so maybe you should concentrate on trying three fruit wines that are probably stocked by some merchant in the neighborhood. These are cherry, plum, and apple.

Of the three, cherry might be the most difficult to locate, but it's worth a scavenger's-hunt effort. Once you've found it, put it on ice for a picnic. Cherry wine, I believe, comes the closest to a normal red table wine as a companion for food.

As for plum wine, look for one imported from Japan, and not just one made in the United States with a Japanese label. A good Japanese plum wine tends to be a bit sweet, but there are few beverages that can compare to it in aroma—full, complex, and sensuous.

Traditionally, plum wine is drunk with Japanese or other Oriental dishes, particularly if they are slightly on the sweet side, and that might be the best way to introduce yourself. A second, and perhaps more enjoyable, way is to have it solo as a dessert wine to serve guests after a fine Saturday evening dinner.

Of course, apple wine is more familiar to us, particularly under the name of cider. Cider is a fall drink—fresh from the crushing with no aging to speak of, spicy and piquant—to be drunk as a cool thirst-quencher.

We are also familiar with cider as the base for hot buttered rum. Sweet apple wine is also a good base for a hot drink—

mulled wine with cloves and cinnamon added for extra spiciness.

Hopefully, you'll find a wine or two you like well enough
to have a permanent place in your wine cellar, perhaps a
dark corner for the forbidden fruits.

Chapter Forty-three

Sparkling wines

IN many ways, Champagne is like soda pop for grownups. Oh sure, a fine vintage Champagne brings up images of elegance and nobility, but generally we think of Champagne as being festive, fun, even a bit raucous. And we drink it primarily at weddings, world championships, and holidays.

Still, in spite of our love for Champagne, we tend to treat it casually and without much differentiation, as though when you've seen one bubble, you've seen them all.

But just as any kid will tell you there are big differences among Coke, Pepsi, and RC, there are also a lot of differences in Champagnes. First of all, most of the stuff that bubbles isn't even Champagne.

The generic should be "sparkling wine," but we in the United States have a habit of stealing French wine names (Burgundy and Chablis are two others). Champagne, of course, comes from the Champagne region of France . . . and everything else isn't, and doesn't.

You don't have to know a whole lot about how sparkling wines are made to know what to look for on the label. Essentially, the gradation from sweet to dry goes *doux, demi-sec, sec* or dry, extra dry, and *brut. Nature* or *natur* means the wine has had no second dosage of sugar and is very crisp. *Méthode champenoise* or "fermented in the bottle" is the traditional and preferred method of making sparkling wine. Beyond that, you only have to know what you like and what you're willing to pay.

But whether your old standby costs $5 or $55, perhaps add some adventure to your life by trying out some bubbles with which you're not familiar.

France. There are quite a number of good vintage Champagnes (those made from a particularly fine year), but they also tend to fetch a good price. If you're curious, try Perrier-Jouet '73, a very nice wine with a pretty bottle to boot. Among the non-vintages, I find Moët et Chandon White Star to my liking—very dry with a carbony, sooty aftertaste. Bollinger Special Cuvée-Brut is fuller and fruitier for about the same price. Lanson is one of the least expensive and most popular and represents a fairly good buy, although it's a bit grapy for my tastes.

French wines not from Champagne are called *vins mousseux.* You might be interested in a sparkling Vouvray from the Loire region, or a brand-name bubbly, such as Kriter Brut de Brut.

(Beware of buying by mistake Côteaux Champenois which comes from the Champagne region and which often has a bottle that looks like Champagne. It is a still or non-sparkling table wine, but many stores stock it in their sparkling wine section.)

Germany. German sparklers go under the name *Sekt*, and a dry one is called *Sekt trocken.* Most of them are made from grapes imported from France, and there are not that many samples available in local stores. One that is has a familiar name—Blue Nun. The last time I tried it, it was a fairly decent wine but with little finesse. One with considerable finesse is the Deinhart Lila, one of the few sparkling wines made from Riesling grapes.

Italy. The stores are literally littered with sparkling wines from Northern Italy, most of them *spumantes* (the Italian word for sparkling wines) from the region of Asti. Although some of them are dry, most bear a touch of sweetness and can be served as a dessert wine. By and large, they are made from the Muscat grape and are a touch cloying. Two of the more popular brands are Zonin and Martini and Rossi.

Israel. The chief export here is Carmel's "The President's Sparkling Wine," which has a very dusty nose and a very vegetal taste. Not exactly unpleasant, but a long way from elegant. I wouldn't recommend it except to seekers of cheap thrills.

Spain. Most Spanish sparkling wines have a distinct herbal, deserty aroma about them which can be interesting as a variation. Some even have the aroma of crushed, dried geranium leaves. They are extremely inexpensive and certainly worth the small investment. Freixenet Carta Blanca is very inexpensive and the spicier, Gewürztraminer-like Cordoniu Blanc de Blanc Brut costs only slightly more.

New York State. There is a myth that sparkling wines are the best of the New York state wines made from foxy American grapes—both faint and false praise. These wines have little elegance and taste too much like grape juice. But the price is right, as most (Taylor, Great Westerns) are quite inexpensive.

California. The West Coast produces some excellent sparkling wines, and my favorite is one made by Frenchmen—Domaine Chandon Blanc de Noir, which has both fruit and elegance. (Since Chandon is French-owned, it does not call its wine Champagne.) The grapes it uses are Pinot Noir (from whence cometh the *blanc de noir*) and Chardonnay, which are what most California and Champagne wine makers use, either blended or as separate varieties. The second name in California is Schramsberg, whose Blanc de Blanc is full, dry, and firm—quite enjoyable, if a bit low in fruit. I have also tried the Cuvée de Pinot Noir, another very good wine.

Hans Kornell (whose *sehr trocken* is popular) is the grand old man of California sparkling wines, but I'm not crazy about his products. I do enjoy Mirrasou, and am so-so about Almadén, whose apricot-colored Eye of the Partridge is pretty to look at, if average to drink. Also look for Korbel.

Russia. Yes, Virginia, there is a Russian "champagne" that even Santa Claus might enjoy. It's called "Nazdorovya" Sparkling Wine, a pleasant wine with an herbal nose and a full, flowery taste.

And, since sparkling wines often do funny things to heads and stomachs the morning after, you might want to stock up on Alka Seltzer—that is, sparkling antacids.

Chapter Forty-four

Zinfandels with a zing

MOST California winemakers cut their teeth on Zinfandel. After all, it is the most widely planted, major red grape in the state, both in terms of acreage and geography. Treat it one way, and it becomes a fruity wine in the Beaujolais style. Another touch, and it becomes a robust, mildly tannic wine in the Cabernet Sauvignon mode. Yet another twist results in a refreshing rosé. Take the skins off quickly, and it becomes a full-bodied "white" wine.

And, fortunately, leave the grapes on the vines for a few extra weeks, and it makes an alcoholic knockout—the zinging, late-harvest Zinfandel. Late picks are a fairly new and very trendy experiment among California wineries, and the reviews are mixed about what this interesting grape has wrought.

For a long time, people thought its origin was the volcanic soils of Hungary, but modern research shows that its forerunner was most likely an obscure, so-so grape from southern Italy aptly named Primivito. Whatever the Zinfandel's origin, it has claimed California as its home. At its best,

Zinfandel can produce a moderately tannic wine that has intense berry flavors which most closely resemble that of blackberries. Many Zinfandels, especially those from Amador County in the Sierra foothills east of Sacramento and some from Sonoma County, also have a rich smell and texture that can best be described as resembling the juices from freshly cooked corn on the cob. The margarine-oil flavor can be distracting, but once one gets beyond it, the result is a rich, full, buttery wine.

Indeed, for years Zinfandel has been a mainstay in the production of the rich California Port-style wine.

Generally the Zinfandel grape—and other grapes for that matter—are picked at the height of their maturity, when the fruit is delectable and before the appearance of the grape starts to deteriorate physically. Very noted exceptions are some white grapes from California, France, and Germany (the Riesling, Sauvignon Blanc, and Chenin Blanc being prime examples), where the clusters are attacked by *botrytis*, a fungus that flourishes in misty morning climates and that leaves a high sugar content in the shriveled, water-robbed grapes.

High sugar in white grapes is normally maintained in the wine. The must is allowed to ferment—transferring sugar into alcohol—only to the point where it reaches stability, perhaps eight to twelve percent. The rest of the sugar remains.

With late-picked Zinfandels, the sugar that results from the additional time on the vine is allowed to ferment almost totally into alcohol with little residual sugar being kept in the wine. Normally, most wines with more than fifteen percent alcohol have gotten that way by being dosed with brandy or straight alcohol.

Not so with late-picked Zinfandels, where the alcohol may rise to more than seventeen percent while maintaining enough sugar for a certain richness. Since the tannin in Zinfandel grapes is mild, these wines are drinkable in a few years, although they may keep and improve for a decade.

Unfortunately, some wineries are still having problems in balancing these huge wines or even in knowing what standard to shoot for.

"Many late-picked Zinfandels are just so much alcoholic tannin water," admits one Washington wine store proprietor. That is true, but others have the lusciousness of non-vintage Port, although it is arguable whether their high price tag can be rationally justified.

Following are descriptions of four such wines which appeared at the height of the late-harvest craze in the late-1970s. Although they might not all be available now, these tasting notes are indicative of the style of wines.

• Monterey Vineyards 1975 Monterey County Zinfandel, December Harvest, Special Selection. "At 14.4 alcohol, this is one of the lightest of the genre, although it is certainly among the more aromatic. It has a beautiful nose—fat, berry, brambly, corn-like. It is full and chewy, but the relative lack of tannin causes it to fade quickly once the bottle is opened."

• Caymus Special Selection 1976 Napa Valley Late Harvest. "I have been constantly disappointed with Caymus wines, which seldom live up to their reputation and price. This one has a sooty nose, almost no body, and is truly like tannin water. Intense airing can raise a hint of fruit but not much, although the blueberry hints that rise are agreeable."

• Napa Wine Cellars 1976 Amador County Zinfandel Selected Late Harvest. "A tarry nose with traces of fruit introduce this complex wine (16.5 alcohol) which is still coming together—fruit, tanning, sugar (1.3 percent) are all prominent. Good drinking now, potentially very good in a few years."

• Ridge California Late Harvest II 1976 Zinfandel. "Primarily from the Esola Ranch of Amador, these grapes have yielded a wine that at first is tannic and closed, but which opens up with airing to a moderately fruity, well-balanced wine with a spicy nose. Although the price is steep it can provide a week of sipping while going through seasonal bottle changes. As I write, it is approaching its autumn—full, smooth, mellow."

Although none of these wines are extraordinary (and none approach the great Amarones of Italy which are somewhat comparable), they are a very enjoyable change of pace. My preferences are the Ridge and Monterey, although the fruity and slightly sweet Napa Wine Cellars is also good.

Unfortunately, some drinkers have relegated these King Kong-like Zinfandels to consumption only with cheese. That certainly is a good match, but I also enjoy sipping these huge wines with meals, although I would never guzzle one. In short, I think they are too rashly—and axiomatically—dismissed as table wines and put in the specialty category.

Not that there is any doubting their alcoholic punch. As wine writer Bob Thompson puts it, "One just coasts from second glass to third to incapacity."

Chapter Forty-five

Just desserts

WE seem to be a country of drinkers who prefer sweetness in everything but wine—soft drinks, coffee, tea. It is true, of course, that we have traditionally preferred a touch of sweetness in our "dry" whites and sprakling wines, but we have never really grasped true dessert wines to our palates.

There are a number of reasons, I suspect. One is that we are like hasty lovers, eager to leave the table (in this case) for a cigarette, a cup of coffee, or an after-dinner brandy.

But the real reason that dessert wines haven't caught on is that most of us think they are cheap, vulgar, and uncouth. They ain't.

Well-made dessert wines will not separate in your glass, leave you gasping for a drink of water, or lower your social status. They might expand your waistline a bit, but they can be cool, clean, and nectary ends to your evening meal.

Generally, they fall into two classes: naturally sweet wines, whose sugar content is elevated by a fungus that robs an overripe grape of excess water, and fortified wines whose alcohol content is considerably more than that of table wines.

Of the former, the most universally acceptable—particularly to new drinkers—are probably the German dessert wines. German wines, especially those from the Mosel, or Moselle, and the Rhine, are at their best when made from the Riesling grape. (If there is no grape name on the label—such as Müller-Thurgau or Sylvaner—then one can hope that the Riesling is responsible for the wine inside.)

These wines are classified according to sugar content. Spätlese means somewhat sweet—a light dessert wine—while Auslese is sweeter and Beerenauslese and Trockenbeerenauslese are considerably sweeter, rarer and hellishly expensive. Settle on a good Auslese from 1976 or 1975 from a reputable vineyard and you'll wonder why you haven't tried it before. The best way to describe the taste is nectary—like ripe peaches and apricots. Incidentally, if the word "trocken" appears on the label, the grape sugar has been converted to alcohol. Hence, it's a dry, not dessert, wine.

California wineries have caught on to grapes that are botrysized—as the fungus-attacked fruit is called—with great success. Again, look for a Riesling or a Chenin Blanc. The label will probably say late-picked or give some other indication of sweetness.

For a completely different taste, try the Hungarian Tokay (or Tokaji) Aszu, which has a more cane-like or molasses taste. It is also clear and clean at its best. "Puttonyos" in ascending order tell the degree of sweetness, and I would recommend three to five (the top) for your enjoyment.

In times past the queen of dessert wines, far outstripping the Germans, was Sauternes from the Bordeaux region of France. It appears to be staging a comeback, and a wine cellar without a few bottles or half-bottles isn't really a cellar. To separate Sauternes mentally from the other dessert wines, think of it as having more of a honey taste with a hint of caramel. If you're already a Sauternes lover, explore the nearby wines of Barsac, Cérons, and Monbazillac, all of which are generally less expensive.

There are other regions that produce botrysized wines, of course, and you may occasionally find one from Côteaux du Layon, such as a Quart de Chaume.

Turning to fortified wines, a friend of mine who is an Irish Catholic, and a drinker by definition, tasted vintage Port not long ago and said for the first time in his life he had a glimpse of heaven. For a long time, this view was mainly seen from Britain, which is responsible for the development of most of the fortified wine trade, including Port.

Fortified wines come from grapes that are, as a rule, inferior for table wines but excellent as a base for stronger ones. Briefly, a raw wine (naturally sweet in the case of Port) is dosed with brandy to raise the alcohol content and kill fermentation, which stops the conversion of grape sugar into alcohol. The wines, generally around 20 percent alcohol, are usually aged for some time. Vintage Port needs fifteen years or so for maturation, while Ruby Port is fruity and ready to drink, and Tawny Port has been mellowed and tamed somewhat. All Port comes from Portugal, but Port-style wines are made around the world, including California, where Ficklin is one of the best.

Port is a full, viscous wine, and one of the few red wines that are desserts. If you think of most wines as being like Jello, then think of Port as Jello mixed with cream cheese to get a textural idea. Port has a slightly nutty taste—a hint of pecans—and should be drunk at room temperatures.

Of course, the real nutty-tasting wine is sherry. As with most other fortified wine, excepting Port, sherry comes in a great variety of sweetness and dryness. The basic wine is dry, again unlike Port, and the sweetness is added, with the dessert varieties being the Olorosos or "creams."

Less popular fortified dessert wines are Madeiras (Malmsey is a sweet grade), Marsala, and Banyuls.

Dessert wines may be had with sweets (there are a few problems, such as chocolate) or sipped alone.

Chapter Forty-six

Brandy: wines that went to heaven

ANY drinkers who pride themselves on recognizing the difference in taste between a Margaux and a Paulliac, or whether a Cabernet Sauvignon is from Rutherford or Alexander Valley, put away their discernment when it comes to brandies. After dinner, it's always a snifter of Cognac by the fire.

Not that there is anything wrong with Cognac. But if, as someone noted, brandy is simply wine that went to heaven, then why content ourselves with the company of only one angel?

Although brandy may come from a fruit other than grapes, the term is historically associated with wine. Indeed, the poetic name "brandywine" simply means "burnt wine," for brandy is wine that is distilled and then, generally, aged in wood.

It is then not surprising that there are as many tastes and nuances in brandy as there are in wine—including price, which runs from a few dollars for cheap California brandy to close to $100 for some Cognac reserves.

And the Cognacs are the most famous, coming from the region of the same name along the Charente River north of Bordeaux. At their best, Cognacs have an intensity of flavor combined with gentle mellowness. The finish can be fiery with a distinctive aftertaste, tangy, and almost salty, surprisingly similar to tequila. The white grapes that make Cognac are undistinguished and very familiar to California jug wine drinkers: Ugni Blanc, Folle Blanche, and Columbard. The color comes from the Limousin oak (a favorite of many American winemakers) which also mellows the raw brandy.

Napoleon popularized the double-distilled Cognac, although neither his name nor the panoply of stars and letters means much to anyone but the distillers, the more prominent and reliable being Bisquit, Rémy Martin, Courvoisier, Hennessy, Martell, and Hine. The word "Champagne" on a label has nothing to do with sparkling wines but rather refers to Grande and Petite Champagne, two of seven Cognac districts.

If Cognac has always marked your brandy limits in France, go south to Gascony near the Spanish border, the home of Armagnac. One of the best is Marquis de Montesquiou, which has a dark woody base to the taste, probably from the black oak of Gascony from which the casks are made. The heavier oak also means Armagnac will age quicker than Cognac. Montesquiou does not have the finesse of most superior Cognacs, yet it is very pliable and almost silky on the tongue with a very dry, fiery, slightly rough finish.

The only other group of brandies which can compete with, and perhaps surpass, Cognac and Armagnac are the "coñacs" of Spain. Perhaps the best is Lepanto from the sherrymaker Gonzales Byass. Spanish brandies are often aged in sherry butts (casks) within a *solera* blending system, and it shows in the taste. Lepanto has a light, dry touch of fino sherry at the front, succumbing to a hint of vanilla (also in the nose), and ending in a fiery, tannic aftertaste—a firm, well-blended brandy. Pedro Domecq's Carlos Primero brand is also a

Spanish frontrunner, but I find his popular Fundador brand to be grapy in the nose and thin on the palate.

A different category of brandies are the Marcs (the "c" is silent) of Champagne, Burgundy (Bourgogne), the Rhône, Italy, and Switzerland. It is truly an acquired taste; perhaps the reason I enjoy Marc so much is that I "acquired" the taste one June night in an outdoor café on the Champs Elysées after a marvelous dinner. Marc is distilled not from young wine but from the *marc* or dregs left over from wine fermentation—seeds, skins, stems—which may account for its pungent (some would say "putrid") nature. Yet it can be delightful.

For example, Marc de Bourgogne from the Ropiteau Frères has the warm dusty nose of a burlap sackful of cracked grain lying in the hot barnyard sun—with a touch of greenness around the edges. It is strong and pungent but smooth with a grainy aftertaste like some whiskeys. Like all brandies, the taste and the nose improve as you swirl it around the snifter, warming it with your hand while giving it air.

The popular Grappa from Italy is also a Marc, and the brand made by Stock, while not as refined as that of Burgundy, is very enjoyable, particularly the fruity nose that wafts up like freshly baked banana-nut bread.

Finally, there are the elegant fruit brandies, generally almost colorless and certainly not to be confused with the cloying, American-made, flavored brandies. Chief among these fruit brandies are the Calvados from Normandy (made from cider), Slivovitz (plums), Framboise (raspberries), Poire (pears), and Kirsch (cherries)—all very delicious. After all, not all of heaven can be reserved for burnt grapes.

Chapter Forty-seven

Marc–a special brandy

WHETHER you're a home winemaker and stomp your grapes to extract the juice, or run a small winery with an old-fashioned wooden barrel press, or head a stainless-steel conglomerate with metallic horizontal presses, there's always the same thing left behind—pomace. Pomace is that unsightly mass of grape skins, seeds, and stems that are left over after the white grape juice or raw red wine has been drawn off.

As nature hates an unused byproduct (this is also known as the Second Law of Capitalism), winemakers have devised a variety of ways to economically get rid of the pomace. One method is to return it to the soil as fertilizer strewn among the vines, a practice common to many small vineyards. The second is to use it as animal feed, particularly cow feed, as is often the case in California. Keep this in mind the next time you bite into a steak.

The third method is Marc, which I discussed briefly in the previous chapter. Or, more properly, *Eau de vie de marc*. Marc (pronounced "mar," and lightly on the "r," please) is a type of brandy that is most popular in France, with a number of supporters in Italy and other countries. Brandy is distilled wine, generally grape wine, but not always, as the large array of fruit brandies on liquor store shelves will attest.

With Marc, we fudge a bit in the definition, as pomace could hardly qualify as wine. And there are those who will argue (more from the palate than the mind) that Marc shouldn't be considered a legitimate brandy, either.

The sad fact is that Marc isn't for everyone. I doubt that many people are enraptured by it after the first sip. But a second sip, and a third sip, and a fourth sip—gradually you get into the spirit of it.

At a recent wine tasting I conducted, for example, I finished the evening by pouring from a bottle of Marc de Bourgogne. Of the two dozen people attending, only three or four bothered to finish the drink. But those three or four replaced the double thimblefuls I poured with generous refills, dutifully wrote down the name of the brand and place of purchase, and were happily nosing their glasses as I left the party. It has that sort of effect on people.

As I mentioned earlier, my first introduction to Marc came one mellow June evening at a sidewalk café on the Champs Elysées, so I was prepared to like it when my friend warned that I probably would not. "It has an odd smell and taste—I don't know how to describe it—it sometimes turns people off," he said.

Well I know how to describe it: "semi-putrid" and "off-barnyard." But one sip led to another, and I am still drinking it. More precisely, Marc has a wet-straw nose and taste that one often associates with the rough-hewn grain taste of some whiskeys. It is just this earthiness, this grain-like quality, that causes many bourbon and rye drinkers to latch onto Marc.

Some of the finest Marc comes from Burgundy (Marc de Bourgogne), and a bottle I have by Ropiteau Frères reminds me of that dusty smell of burlap feedsacks in the hot country sun. It also has a stem-like taste around the edges, and the finish is firm and definite. Jadot, a famous name in wines, particularly Beaujolais, also imports a Marc de Bourgogne to this country.

The friend who introduced me to Marc lives in Switzerland and loves prowling around wine stores and at doors of wineries in eastern France. At last count, he had more than thirty varieties, the best of which are from Burgundy, the Rhône, and particularly Champagne. The latter I will have to take on faith, for I have not tasted it.

That is one of the problems for Marc lovers who live here, not Europe. The concoction is seldom available in any but the larger wine and liquor stores. If you can't find French Marc, however, then try the Italian version called Grappa. The Grappa that I have tasted, principally from Stock, is grapier and rougher. Although, when warmed by the hands in a snifter, this brandy can have the appealing aroma of freshly baked banana bread.

As far as I know, no one in California commercially manufactures Marc, but I'm sure that sometime soon our brethren of the Golden West will get around to that challenge. Marc de Napa may be just a few years away.

If you are already accustomed to Marc through foreign travels, there is a variant you might enjoy. That is "Lie," a brandy or eau de vie made not from freshly pressed pomace, but from the sediment that gradually falls to the bottom of the barrel as the wine ages. The bottle I have is simply labeled Vielle Lie du Prieure and comes in a furniture-polish bottle with a screw cap top.

Manufactured by the winemakers of Geneva, it is about 80 proof and has a deceptively light foretaste that is wiped away by a rough, straw-like finish. Again, I should warn that Lie is not for everyone, either, not even Marc drinkers.

My advice with Marc—or Lie—is to try it, even if you probably won't like it.

PART SEVEN
Unraveling the Mysteries of Wine Making

Chapter Forty-eight

How wines are made

WHAT would you say if you heard some winemaker in Southern California had performed a sex change operation on perfectly good Pinot Noir grapes, added adulterants to the raw wine, hyped it up with bubbles, and put it on the market? Call in Ralph Nader and the Grape Aides?

And what if another grower picked his grapes at the perfect moment, but then left them to shrivel until all the *faux* snow under the Los Angeles Christmas trees had been swept away? Would you drink wine made from them?

Or if another vintner added strawberry juice to his vat and put this off-pink wine next to the Cabernet in your wine store? Call out the boycotts!

Change around the locales a bit, and you have Champagne in the first case, Amarone in the second case, and "pop wines" in the third case. The first two wine drinkers love, and the last one they despise as kid stuff.

What got me thinking about all this was that I was sitting around the other day sipping on some fine 1971 Amarone and reading a magazine advertisement for Shogun—not the book, but a new drink from Japan that is reported to be a combination of grape wine ("grape" wine being redundant to most of us purists) and rice wine, or Sake.

Looking for a moral, four thoughts came to me: (1) Sometimes we get too carried away with the idea of getting maximum varietal characteristics from a wine, that is, making the wine conform to "classic" standards according to the grape, at the risk of tolerating experimentation; (2) If some of the experiments that give us some of our best wines were being carried out today, most of us wine writers would laugh at them; (3) Some experiments fail, aesthetically, and should be laughed at—"pop wines" being one of them; and (4) Many people might appreciate the wines they drink a little bit better if they understood some of the things that go into winemaking after the grapes are picked.

Let's go with No. 4.

The next time you want a bottle of moderately priced dry white wine, buy a bottle of Muscadet, making certain it says *sur lie* on the label. When you chill and pour the wine, see if you can get a slight yeasty taste with a little frizziness on the tongue. If you do, then that's the result of the winemaker's deciding not to rack his wine—that is clean out the crud from the bottom of the barrel—as often as most winemakers do. What could be criticized as sloppy winemaking results in a delightful, fruity variation.

Or think about the sherries, Ports, and Madeiras you drink. Actually these wines exist because of an early need for preservatives. The preservative used in centuries past for the long haul of Spanish, Portuguese, and even early Bordeaux to England was alcohol in the form of brandy and heavy, concentrated red wine to protect (and change) more delicate, natural wines. With the advent of corks, and modern sterilization techniques, this dosing is no longer necessary. But who wants to stop now?

Champagne? The real stuff from France is also dosed with sugar *after* the raw wine is made and bottled. Why? Well, this causes a second fermentation which causes carbon dioxide which causes pressure which makes the cork fly across the room and the bubbles flow. And, of course, some of the best of this white wine is made from red grapes whose pigmented skin is thrown away before it can color the wine.

Amarone? Buy a bottle of five-to-ten-year-old Recioto della Valpolicella Amarone and taste what a really intense, strong, macho red wine can be like. The intensity comes from grapes turned into raisins and then fermented. Recioto without the word Amarone indicates a sweeter wine, so make certain of what you're getting. In California, of course, the worst insult to a wine man is to tell him he's using raisin grapes.

Like fruity Beaujolais? It may taste fresh and fruity partly because of the Gamay grape and partly because of carbonic maceration. Normally, grapes are crushed so they will ferment easily. With carbonic maceration, only some of the grapes are crushed, generally due to the weight of grapes on top. This causes a slow fermentation that can intensify flavor (if not longevity), as some of the grapes literally burst with pleasure.

Wonder about that undertaste in your Chardonnay? Could it be the oak casks? Is that scorched taste in your Petite Sirah a result of heated must (grape juice) to enhance fermentation and give better coloring? Folle Blanche never tasted so good before? Maybe you can thank cold fermentation for that.

Finally, have you ever seen the term *vinho de torna viagem* on a Port or Madeira? Probably not, as that refers to the abandoned Portuguese custom of loading barrels onto ships and carrying them to the East Indies and back just for the ride. Folks even said it made the wine taste better.

And you thought Congress came up with all the good ideas.

Chapter Forty-nine

Why wines are blended

WE Americans like to think of ourselves as a homogeneous people with homogeneous ideals. We still
call ourselves a nation of immigrants, a melting pot of colors,
languages, religions, shapes, sizes, and sexes.

We even think of our pets in the same terms. In the
movies, it's the mongrel dog—a spunky mutt—who rushes
into the burning house to save the family, never the pure-
bred Afghan hound. The alley cat is depicted as streetwise,
but lovable, while the Persian is beautiful, but vain and
dumb.

Whether with people or animals, ethnic purity—to coin a
phrase—has never had too much going for it in American
popular sentiment. Indeed, such terms as "royalty" or "blue
blood" are often spoken in disdainful tones.

Yet we have the opposite sentiment, it seems, when we
are dealing with wines. The *ne plus ultra* is the wine made
from grapes of 100 percent of the same variety, picked in the
same vineyard at the same time. And the whole matter of
wine labeling has some wine fanatics seeing purple, as they

200

would not call a wine by a certain name, say Chenin Blanc, unless it were nearly 100 percent Chenin Blanc.

Mike Grgich, winemaker and co-proprietor of Grgich Hills winery in the Napa Valley, states that view as strongly as possible. "Blending is done to improve the wine. If you can't make a top varietal wine, then you season it with something else. I'm trying to make perfect varietal wines." Of course, Grgich is 100 percent right in some ways (and he does make beautiful varietal wines) and 50 percent right and 50 percent wrong in other ways.

The whole matter of blending or "mongrelizing" wines is something worth looking into and understanding for the serious drinker. Wines have been blended almost from the beginning of time with both great and disastrous results. For example, Champagne, sherry, Bordeaux, Châteauneuf-du-Pape, Chianti, and Hermitage are all blended wines, although they are not all blended in the same way or for the same reasons. And—at their best—all are superior, even great wines.

Why? Well, as Grgich begins, blending is done to improve the wine. A wine from a single source that has not been tampered with may be too alcoholic, too acidy, too anemic in color, or too anemic in body, just to cite a few problems. These deficiencies may be corrected—or avoided entirely—by any of a different method of blending. Let's review a few:

• *Blending of vintages.* Not every year is a good year, so blending of different vintages—or harvests—is done to get a certain level of quality or evenness of style. Two examples, though quite different, are Champagne and sherry.

Except for vintage Champagne made from a great year, most Champagne is a mixture of new wine (say from 1979) and an older wine (say from 1978). This works at its best when one vintage can make up for the deficiencies of another and vice versa. Choosing the right amount from each vintage and even the vintages themselves challenges the skills of the winemaker or wine ager. Slightly different is sherry.

where many vintages are integrated through a series of barrels with new wine being added at top and aged wine being taken off at the bottom.

Mixing of vintages of table wines is rare in California due to labeling restrictions.

• *Blending of grapes.* "Blending for the purpose of 'thinning' a varietal is not done," says Richard Arrowood, the brilliant winemaker at Château St. Jean and a general advocate of 100 percent varietals. But, as Arrowood recognizes, there may be exceptions, and the Cabernet Sauvignon is one of them.

Even though Cabernet is recognized as perhaps the best black (red) wine grape in the world, it is generally blended with small amounts of Merlot, Cabernet Franc, and other grapes in its most famous domain—Bordeaux. Why? To soften the harshness of the tannin of the grapes, either for purposes of taste or to cut down on time of aging. Many California winemakers are against this practice, however, arguing that 100 percent Cabernet is better than blended.

In some areas, all wines are blended. Most wine drinkers would not recognize the names of the four or so grapes that go into the making of Chianti or many of the thirteen that can go into Châteauneuf-du-Pape. The legendary Hermitage has the sturdy Syrah as its backbone, but is softened and given fragrance by a white grape, Viognier.

"We are trying to get a good variety of Viognier," says Walter Schug, winemaker of Joseph Phelps, the only California concern to make a true Syrah wine. "But we have been experimenting with other white varieties for three years." So far, Chenin Blanc has proved to be the best substitute.

• *Blending of vineyards.* The same variety of grape grown in different climates with different soils and growing conditions will taste differently.

"It's sometimes possible to take two vineyards—say from

Paso Robles and the Napa Valley—and blend the grapes to make the wine more complex or better," says winemaker Paul Draper of Ridge. "But if you have fine wines to begin with, I wouldn't blend. I'd rather know that this wine resulted from what was happening this year in this area."

Nevertheless, blending by vineyards is probably the chief form of blending among premium California wineries, where estate bottling is of less concern than it is in Europe.

• *Blending of cuvées.* Sometimes there are advantages in mixing the wine made from grapes picked early and those picked late, which may have different acid and alcohol content. Maryland winemaker Hamilton Mowbray, for example, did that with some of his 1980 white varietals.

• *Blending of fermentation methods.* This is rarer, but one case involves Monteviña Vineyards of Amador County where Cary Gott says, "If a lighter wine is desired, I may add some wine made by whole berry or carbonic maceration (the grapes are not crushed) methods to wine made by the normal (crushed grapes) method."

There are also different techniques of blending, regardless of the reason. In Bordeaux and elsewhere, some vineyards will have different types of grape vines growing in the same vineyards. The grapes are picked together—blended in the basket, so to speak—and fermented *en masse.* Others, such as Phelps with its Syrah, will do the picking and crushing separately and then blend in the fermenter.

The practice in Bordeaux is also for a shipper to buy raw wines from different growers and then blend them in the aging barrel and "elevate" or "educate" them, again looking for a consistent taste from year to year. This is also referred to as "marrying" wines. Most shippers' wines (such as B & G, Mouton Cadet) are made in this manner.

Few wines are blended after they have been finished, that is after filtering or fining, as the reaction could cause additional clouding or precipitating.

But back to Mike Grgich. Blending is done to improve an inferior wine, as he says. But it is dubious to say that even the best Cabernet or Sauvignon Blanc would not be improved by blending. A little bit of mutt can often give the best pure-bred an extra touch of character.

Chapter Fifty

The cask system: the role of oak in aging

A few years ago, a friend of mine who had moved—temporarily—to California, a hard-liquor man, returned a born-again wine drinker. He brought back as much of his wine cellar as possible, even stowing the best bottles in his wife's luggage.

One bottle he was particularly proud of was a David Bruce Chardonnay—I forget the vintage—and he quickly arranged a small dinner party to showcase his prize. At that time, I had not tasted a Bruce Chardonnay, but I had heard that Bruce was to oak aging as Sammy Davis is to Cream Concord.

The Bruce held no surprises. The main course of chicken was unmercifully flogged by the overpowering oak taste of the wine. Neither were toothpicks needed later; it was as if there was a splinter in every glass.

If David Bruce and his dyed-in-wood California counterparts did nothing else, they raised the wine drinking public's consciousness to wood in wine. It is an interesting subject to contemplate. The first winemakers to use wood as cooperage—that is, storage vessels—probably had little regard for what it did for the taste of the wine.

The method of the storing and aging of wine in huge casks first became a science of sorts in the 1800s. It was learned that while oak protected wine from rapid oxidation, it still allowed the wine to breathe a bit and that the wood helped round off rough edges.

Within limits, wood can add some age to wines, although age is largely a factor of the amount of tannin put in the wine by the presence of grape skins, stems, and seeds or pips (particularly if the pips are crushed) during fermentation. Too much wood can also tame a wine and shorten its life. For that reason, vintage Port stays in the wood for only two years.

The wine does not lie idle during these two or three years. The casks are topped off as wine evaporates, solids are carried to the bottom by the addition of gelatin or other substances (egg whites are traditional), and the wine is transferred or racked from one cask to another so that the dregs can be removed.

There are other considerations: which kind of oak to use (surprisingly, sherry is aged on American oak while many California wines are aged on French or German oak), and how much sulphur must be used to sterilize the barrel without harming the wine that will mature in the casks.

But this is history. What the California oak debate is about is how should oak affect the taste of a wine. Traditionalists argue that a little is good but that too much, particularly in whites such as Chardonnay, will hide the varietal taste, which they consider all important. Additionally, smaller wineries often ferment Chardonnay on oak for added complexity.

There is no doubt that oak does impart a taste. In some mellow red or white wines, you may note a slight vanilla taste. That is oak. In some California red wines (and in some Europeans, as well), such as the Petite Sirah, you may discover a slightly "cooked" taste. That may be oak. In white wines, the taste of oak may appear subtly—a slight tingling, bubbly, tartness on the tongue—or boldly—an almost syrupy heaviness that will be familiar to anyone who has ever chewed on an oak splinter while splitting firewood.

Obviously, there is no "correct" taste in oak, or anything else with wine, for that matter. There is often a consensus among those who are familiar with wine, but even that is lacking in the oak debate.

The lines aren't so finely drawn with reds, but gradually you can learn to pick up the difference in taste that is attributable to the wood and not the grape.

Then you can form your own philosophy as to how much oak is enough—and join the appropriate splinter group.

Chapter Fifty-one

The myth of estate-bottling

REMEMBER back when you were a mere tad taking your first course in wine appreciation and how you immediately started looking at all the pretty labels in the wine primer? And do you remember how the arrow pointed to the words "Estate-Bottled," and the caption said "indication of quality"?

Now that you're a tad bigger, do you still believe it, the same way that you believe that natural is better than artificial, that winning is the only thing, and that you never draw to an inside straight?

Then how do you account for Robert Young, Martha's Vineyard, Belle Terre, and Hunter Ranch? As many of you know, those are names of famous California vineyards whose grapes have produced great wines, prize-winning wines. And not a one of them estate-bottled.

The point is not that estate-bottling is bad, of course, but that it's not always an indication even of drinkability, and it certainly isn't the only way to produce a fine wine, as the old premise would have it.

Estate-bottling is essentially a European concept historically devised to ensure quality and provide truth in labeling. If a wine is château-bottled or estate-bottled, then we know that some shipper or other middleman is not buying grapes or raw wine from a famous region or vineyard and cutting them with lesser juices. The grower and winemaker work for the same owner or are actually one and the same.

Of course, even in France blended wine was, and is, the order of the day in some regions, such as Champagne and Alsace.

In California, things are never quite so easy. Under pressure from such writer-savants as the late Frank Schoonmaker, varietal bottling became the tag of quality. We were perfectly happy to see on the label something like "Napa Valley Chardonnay." Initially, we didn't really care whether or not the winery was located in the same field as the grapes, although often that was the case.

Nevertheless, there are those who still believe the ideal situation is to have the winery and the vineyard adjacent with one central figure supervising both the vines and the vats. Some of the better wines are made this way. For example, a small quality winery such as Enz in San Benito County can pick the grapes within sight of the crusher and have the must in the fermenter only minutes after picking. Even such relatively large wineries as Robert Mondavi, which buys many grapes, still have large contiguous vineyards.

However, it is increasingly difficult for new wineries to buy large tracts of good grape-growing land (or to buy an existing vineyard) and go into estate-bottling. One exception is the new Jordan Vineyard in Sonoma, which intends to have only estate-bottled Cabernet Sauvignon and Chardonnay. Obviously, this takes considerable initial investment plus considerable operating funds while one waits three to six years for the vines to reach even modest maturity.

In most cases, a new winery will simply buy grapes from reliable growers, at least on a temporary basis. Ridge, particularly famous for its Zinfandels, continues to purchase approximately 80 percent of its grapes although it owns the adjacent Monte Bello Vineyard and supervises two other nearby holdings. The newer, smaller Grgich Hills Winery makes excellent Chardonnays and Rieslings from carefully bought grapes.

One of the reasons for estate-bottling has been to ensure not only that the grapes *are* from a particular region—less of a problem perhaps in California than in scandal-ridden France—but also that they are grown in a manner to get maximum quality from the vines. Not everyone agrees.

"Sometimes, it's better not to own the vines," maintains Roy Thomas of Monterey Peninsula Winery. "That way there is no temptation to overproduce." Maximum fruit generally means minimum quality. Therefore, judicious pruning is always necessary, and Thomas believes a winery can be more demanding when it buys grapes from someone else than it might be if it grew the grapes itself.

"We have most of our growers under contract and have as much quality control as most wineries that own vineyards," he says. "Additionally, we have a lease-sharing program to help protect everyone in case of crop failure. Besides, we're so small that we have the pick of what we want down here (in Monterey County)."

Possibly the best winery in California, especially for whites, is Château St. Jean, which buys 95 percent of its grapes, primarily through long-term contract.

"Whether you have estate-bottling or contracts with growers, the goal is the same," says Château St. Jean president Arthur Hemphill, "and that is to get the winery interested in the growing conditions. When you move into estate-bottling, you make a commitment to a particular piece of ground. But it's the same idea with long-term grower contracts."

St. Jean has thus latched onto such excellent vineyards as Belle Terre and Robert Young and helps oversee the quality control at these and other contract holdings.

In addition to quality control considerations, proponents of estate-bottling cite the fact that bought grapes can be damaged in shipment or lose something over long hauls. Two good wineries that buy grapes have different approaches to overcoming these potential problems.

Owner Joseph Phelps of the winery of the same name maintains, "If it's done right the grapes will not deteriorate in shipping. Even with white grapes, they will come out okay if picked 'cool' and if shipped in small bins. We're not talking about bulk grapes," he reminds. "If you're paying for quality grapes, then there is incentive to justify proper handling."

Winemaker Peter Stern of Turgeon & Lohr says his firm has a slightly different approach. "We do the crushing in the field and ship the must (crushed grapes and juice) back to the winery," he says. Most of his firm's holdings are in Monterey while the fermentation tanks are in downtown San José. "We put the must in a tanker and fill it up with carbon dioxide and add sulphur dioxide. Really, the quality control is so fantastic that way."

Mirrasou and Wente also field crush, a technique not that dissimilar to the methods used in the Champagne district of France.

However, while many California wineries are crossing estate lines and paying less attention to how close the winery and grapes are, the vineyards are nevertheless getting more attention on the label. Ridge and Château St. Jean are particularly known for telling the buyer not only the variety, but also the vineyard designation. That practice is growing, and even Robert Mondavi is considering putting vineyard designation on some of his Cabernets—ToKalon—even though he owns the vineyard.

"Growers have egos, too," Thomas of Monterey Peninsula says. "If they sell their grapes to a bulk winery, they never know whose wine it is. With vineyard designation, they can eventually find out what their wine tastes like."

Chapter Fifty-two

You as a winemaker

MOST of us have house wines, fairly ordinary but dependable favorites, that can go with a variety of foods. A Côtes du Rhône for a red, perhaps, and a Soave for a white.

But how would you like to have a house wine that is really a house wine—one that you made yourself?

Yes, it can be a bit of an affectation, like a coffee table book on the influence of minimal art on the Eskimo, and, no, it probably won't be all that outstanding to drink.

However, it is fairly easy to make a case or two of decent, drinkable wine for around $50. And you can obtain a better understanding of commercial wines in the process.

For the past three years, I have made two cases each of Chardonnay and Chambourcin (a red hybrid variety) from grapes I picked myself in a Delaware vineyard that a friend of mine owns. I'm not a tinkerer, so I've put only modest efforts into the venture, and the results have been modest wines of above jug-wine level.

My friend's vineyard is only one of a string throughout the United States where you can buy fresh grapes for wine-

212

making. Table grapes from the supermarket are not very good for winemaking, and they're too expensive. An easier alternative is to buy a concentrate at a wine hobby store, but that takes some of the fun out of it.

Whichever way, the basics of winemaking are simple. Grapes have sugar, and, when the grapes are crushed, naturally occurring yeasts will cause the sugar to ferment and make alcohol. Air is the ally and enemy of winemaking—too much causes vinegar, but some is needed to mature the wine. Everything else flows from this.

Essential equipment (other than grapes) in the beginning are a commercial yeast for better fermentation, Campden tablets (sulphur) to prevent spoilage, and a large plastic trash can. The yeast and sulphur are added to the crushed grapes which are then dumped in the can to ferment, with a loosely fitted plastic trash bag acting as a lid. If the grapes are white, first press out all the juice and throw the skins away before fermenting. With red grapes, keep the skins on a day or so for color and tannin.

After this seething mass has quit bubbling in a week to 10 days, the raw wine is siphoned via plastic tubing into a carboy, jugs, or other large containers for settling and secondary fermentation. Try to leave as much of the solid material behind as possible. A small, plastic gas lock, available at wine hobby stores, is capped on top of the carboy and filled with water to allow carbon dioxide to escape without letting oxygen in.

After fermentation slows down in the ensuing weeks, the wine is racked once or twice in the winter and early spring. Racking consists of siphoning the wine into another container so that the lees or dregs can be removed and the wine allowed to clarify. Around April or May, the wine is ready for bottling, either in screw-cap containers or a corked bottle. Corks and a corker are inexpensive.

Of course, home winemaking can be very complex if you do like to tinker. When do you pick the grapes to get maximum sugar and acid balance? How long do you want to keep the skins in the must? Do you want to blend varieties? What kind of yeast is best? Do you want to chaptalize: that is, add sugar? How much sulphur is enough to protect the wine without giving it a bad taste? Do you want to age the new wines in casks before bottling? Have you considered cold fermentation? And do you want to stop fermentation to leave some sweetness?

An excellent place to begin learning is with Phillip Wagner's *Grapes into Wine* which is as good a book as I've seen on amateur winemaking. Next, check out one of the area wine hobby shops for equipment. Finally, start making calls to see which vineyards, stores, or markets have wine grapes to sell.

There are Federal regulations on how much wine you can make, and you are not allowed to sell it or, technically, give it away. If you have questions, call the Bureau of Alcohol, Tobacco, and Firearms in the Treasury Department.

Then, some time, some winter, as you savor a glass of your own raw wine during racking, it will occur to you. Who needs all those tomato plants and sweet peas in the back yard, you'll ask. No one, of course.

Your garden is just taking up space where grape vines could be growing.

Afterword

After more than 50 chapters, it appears that we should have exhausted the subject of wine.

But, of course, we have not.

It is often said that wine is "a living thing, constantly changing." So is its study. After four years of writing a weekly column on wine, I find people are surprised that I have no problem thinking of new topics week in, week out. As a matter of fact, I always have a backlog of thirty or so ideas that is constantly being replenished. There is no need to repeat subjects.

For example, as this book is being completed, I am doing research on or writing stories about topics that will greatly influence your and my wine drinking both now and in the future—new scientific methods in the vineyard, the French invasion of California, the trend in Germany from dessert wines to dry or "trocken" table wines, the export market of Europe and the Far East that is being intrigued by California's finest.

Then there are practical topics—how do you stock a summer wine cellar, how do you judge the earthy wines of Monterey, which wine society should you join, how do you prepare for a visit to a winery?

And we can always look into history—what has happened to the wines and vineyards that the ancients swore by? What did the Napa Valley wine business look like through the eyes of Robert Louis Stevenson?

Recently, tired but still excited, I was reflecting on the simplicity of wine and the complexity of its world as I was leaving the Napa Valley after a long week of interviewing and tasting.

After almost a hundred wines tasted—including harsh young barrel samples—my tongue felt a little ripped from the alcohol and tannin. Yet I could have tasted more. It is easy to see, I thought as I drove toward the Airport Holiday Inn, how people can become so wrapped up, so serious about the topic of wine.

Carrying wines yet to be tasted and notes not yet deciphered, I checked into my room, then walked toward the bar. A sip of Champagne before dinner? Yet another boutique Chardonnay? Or, for a change of pace, a fino sherry?

Everything, even wine, has its place, I decided.

"Jack Daniels on the rocks, please."

Suggested reading

Guides

These books are excellent references to carry while traveling and to carry with you to the wine stores.

Johnson, Hugh. *Hugh Johnson's Pocket Encyclopedia of California Wines.* New York: Simon and Schuster, 1977.

Olken, Charles, Roby, Norman, and Singer, Earl. *The Connoisseurs' Handbook of California Wines.* New York: Knopf, 1980.

Basic Volumes

Four books to be stranded in a desert vineyard with.

Blacker, Elwyn; Cooper, Brian; and Peppercorn, David. *Drinking Wine: A Complete Guide with Ratings.* New York: Harbor House Books, 1979.

Broadbent, Michael. *Wine Tasting: Enjoying and Understanding.* London: Christie's Wine Publications, 1979.

Johnson, Hugh. *The World Atlas of Wine.* New York: Simon and Schuster, 1976.

Schoonmaker, Frank. *Schoonmaker's Encyclopedia of Wine.* New York: Hastings House, 1978.

Specialized Reading

If you're really hooked, some books tell you everything from how to make wine to how to enjoy it.

Adams, Leon. *The Wines of America.* New York: McGraw-Hill, 1980.

Balzer, Robert Lawrence. *Wines of California.* New York: Abrams, 1978.

Cross, Gilbert; and Wallace, Forrest. *The Game of Wine.* New York: Harper & Row, 1977.

Grossman, Harold J.; and Lembeck, Harriet. *Grossman's Guide to Wines, Beers and Spirits.* 6th rev. ed. New York: Scribner's, 1977.

Hillman, Howard. *The Diner's Guide to Wines.* New York: Dutton, 1978.

Johnson, Hugh; and Thompson, Robert. *The California Wine Book.* New York: Morrow, 1976.

Wagner, Phillip. *Grapes into Wine: The Art of Winemaking in America.* New York: Knopf, 1976.

Wildman, Frederick, Jr. *Wine Tour of France: A Convivial Guide to French Vintages and Vineyards.* New York: Random House, 1976.